PUB W.
IN HAMP
and the I.O.W.

Forty Circular Walks

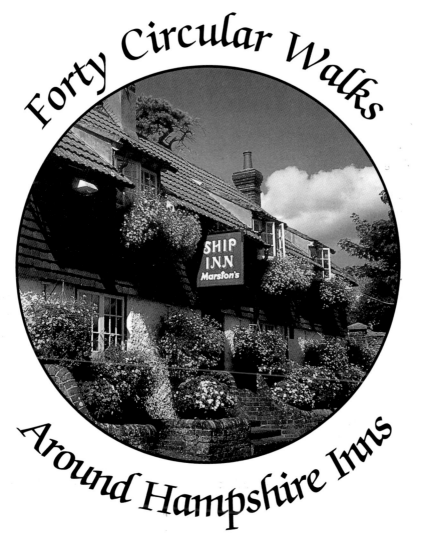

Around Hampshire Inns

Mike Power

"This is not the sort of book that big hikers would need. It is aimed at introducing people for the first time, to the sheer pleasure of walking"
— Paul Allen. Southern Evening Echo May '90

Other publications in the series

"Pub Walks in Dorset"
"Forty More Pub Walks in Dorset"
"Pub Walks in Somerset"
"Pub Walks in West Sussex"
"Pub Walks in East Sussex"
"Pub Walks in Devon"
"Pub Walks in Cornwall"
"Pub Walks in the New Forest"
"Pub Walks in Hardy's Wessex"

1st edition - published March '90
2nd edition - published March '91
3rd edition - published September '91
4th edition - published May '93
5th edition - published June '99

Acknowledgements

I am indebted to David Hancock for his invaluable assistance checking the majority of the walks and pub reports for this new edition.

© Power Publications

1 Clayford Avenue
Ferndown
Dorset. BH22 9PQ

ISBN 1 898073 17 1

Publisher's note

Whilst every care has been taken to ensure that all the information contained in this book is correct neither the authors or publishers can accept any responsibility for any inaccuracies that occur.

Front Cover: The Ship Inn, Owslebury.
Rear Cover: Red Lion, Chalton.
Photographs: Mike Power/Bonita Toms.

INTRODUCTION

I wrote my first book, *Pub Walks in Dorset*, hoping it would appeal to a few people but never expecting it to be a commercial success. Many other excellent publications too often leave you stranded, tired thirsty and miles from civilisation. If nothing else but the thought of a cool refreshing drink, a comfortable chair and a bite to eat is enough to push tired limbs in time for last orders.

From my correspondence it is clear I have introduced walking to a whole new sector of the population, both young and old and entire families. I hope this second book will be equally well received, both by regular and new walkers alike.

I have to admit that in the past, apart from visiting the New Forest, I have only driven through Hampshire and always thought of it as a fast and furious county with many large towns, linked by busy roads and even busier motorways. I happily admit to being wrong – Hampshire is a beautiful county of vast rolling countryside, pretty villages, lovely unspoilt pubs and endless miles of well-maintained public footpaths. The transformation from tarmac to tranquility happens almost as soon as you leave the main highways. I speak of course as an outsider, although only just; Hampshire Hogs I'm sure are fully aware of their beautiful heritage.

All the inns featured in this book are in rural locations. The walks, all circular and varying from 1¾ miles to 6 miles, are explained in detail with an accompanying sketch map. Some are easy, some are more challenging but most are well-marked and easy to follow. On the rare occasion when you want to walk but not visit the inn we would respectfully ask you not to use their car park; in most cases one can park close by and where possible, we have listed these areas.

It has now been proved that walking is extremely good for you, it is also safe providing a few simple rules are observed. Try to always wear suitable clothing, strong waterproof boots are best but any stout shoes will do as long as the weather is fine. If possible take an Ordnance Survey map of the area and if you are walking in misty conditions, or in the evening, a compass and torch could prove useful. I always take a walking stick; it is ideal for clearing brambles and can help pull your walking companion up a steep slope, it can also act as a probe to test the stability of the ground ahead and, probably most important of all, can be waved to deter animals.

When walking along country lanes without pavements remember to keep to the right-hand side of the road. Close and fasten all gates. Keep dogs under control and always on a lead where there are livestock. Never pick wild flowers or dig up the plants. If we all play our part the landowners will do likewise.

Rights of way do not cease to exist just because they are obstructed or impossible to use. On the 13th August 1990 a new "Rights of Way Act" became law, primarily to deal with and clarify the problem faced by walkers confronting footpaths that have been ploughed over, covered with crops or are just impossible to follow. Under the new act the occupier of the land must make good the surface within 14 days of the first disturbance, or within 24 hours for subsequent operations such as hoeing or ridging up, etc. It must have a minimum width of one metre for a footpath and two metres for a bridleway, and the exact line of the path must be apparent on the ground. You should report any problems you find to the relevant authority. Where the right of way crosses a field with growing crops you are entitled to follow the route even if it means treading on the crop. If the path is blocked you are entitled to remove just enough of the obstruction to get by but not to cause willful damage.

We enjoyed all these walks, we hope you will as well.

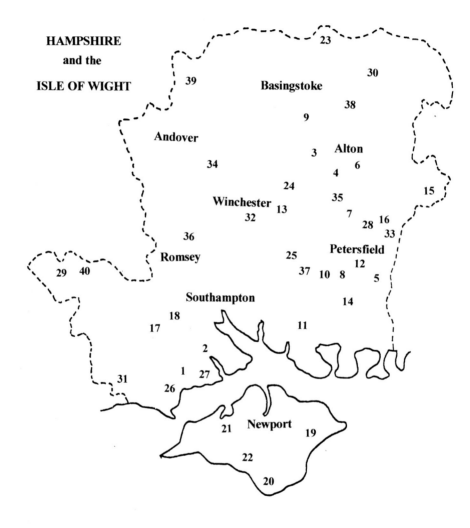

HAMPSHIRE
and the
ISLE OF WIGHT

23

30

39

Basingstoke

38

9

Andover

3   Alton

34   4   6

24

Winchester   35   15

32   13   7

28   16

33

36   25   Petersfield

Romsey   12

29   40   37   10   8   5

14

Southampton

18

17   11

2

1   27

31   26

21   Newport   19

22

20

The Hobler, Battramsley

It has been said that a pub is as good as its landlord - this is never more true than at the lovely 'Hobler'. It is not a smart pub but it is a great pub; the friendly landlord ensures it stays that way. The building is over 400 years old and was once a combined butcher's, baker's shop and pub. It is named after a hobler, a man who would hoble horses by tying its front legs together so it can feed but not run off. It was on Setley Plain that such a man would look out to sea for approaching enemy ships. He would light a beacon, mount his horse and ride to Winchester to warn of the risk of invasion.

Inside the inn are two separate bar areas with wooden floors and mats. Around the walls are cases of stuffed animals, a large bookcase and various farm tools. Furnishings are simple but adequate. At the rear is a large beer garden with tables, chairs and picnic benches.

The bar is extremely well stocked. Three real ales include Flowers IPA, Wadworth 6X and a regularly-changing guest beer. There are over 75 different malt whiskies and a good wine list.

The inn is well known for its good food. The regularly-changing menu includes snacks like filled jacket potatoes, ploughman's lunches and paté with garlic bread, and hearty main meals like 'pork char-su' (belly pork marinated in honey, soy sauce and sherry); 'liver Italian' (cooked in red wine, mint, onions and tomatoes), steak and kidney pie, char-grilled venison steaks, sea bass with a lemon butter sauce, or squid cooked with garlic, cockles and mussels. On fine sunny Sundays there is a barbeque in the garden.

Open from 10.30am till 2.30pm (3pm Sat) and from 6pm till 11pm.

Telephone (01590) 623291.

The inn is situated beside the A337 Brockenhurst to Lymington road, 2 miles south of Brockenhurst.

Approx. distance of walk: 3 miles. O.S. Map No. 196 SZ 307/991.

The inn has a large car park.

A short but enjoyable country walk combining peaceful lanes, wooded paths and forest tracks. It is generally easy going and ideal for the whole family. For a longer walk you can link this one with the walk from the Fleur-de-Lys at Pilley. Both walks cross in Boldre at the Red Lion, another pub well worth a visit.

1. Cross the road from the inn and go over the stile on the right-hand side of a house. Follow the narrow path to a further stile and enter forestry land. Continue ahead to a gravel drive and turn left, following it past several houses, then bear right and shortly cross the railway bridge. The track bears left, passes more houses and eventually reaches a lane.

2. Turn left under the railway bridge and follow the lane back to the main road. Turn right then immediately left into Rope Hill and walk down the road (can be busy) to the Red Lion in Boldre. Turn left and continue along the narrow lane for some distance, turning left when you reach Lower Sandy Down Lane. Pass a few houses then take the waymarked footpath on the left, opposite the second narrow lane on the right.

3. Walk down through the trees, over the stream at the bottom and head uphill on a defined path through the field to a stile in the top left-hand corner. Enter another field and keep the hedge on your left to reach a further stile, then follow the narrow woodland path back to a small gate beside the inn and giving access to the A337. Turn left for the pub entrance and car park.

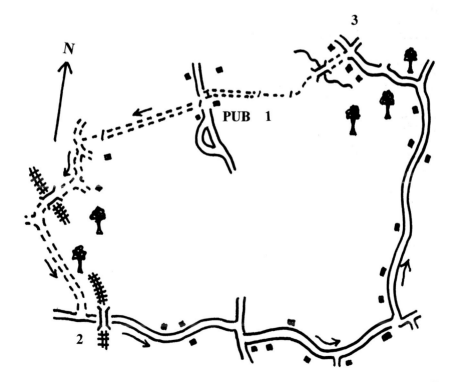

The Montagu Arms Hotel, Beaulieu

Strictly speaking the Montagu Arms, a charming creeper-clad building, is a hotel, but is included because of its unique position at the head of the Beaulieu river, opposite Palace House, and the fact that Monty's, an adjoining bar and bistro, is a very good place to eat and drink. The decor is contemporary and relaxing and the furnishings comfortable.

The Montagu Arms, being a free house, offers the excellent local ale Ringwood Best and a regularly-changing guest beer on handpump. Half a dozen wines are available by the glass.

The bistro-style menu offers an interesting choice of light dishes and more substantial meals. Typical starters include mussels with white wine and parsley and goat's cheese salad with red and yellow peppers, while imaginative snacks range from Caesar salad with grilled chicken, Greek salad, char-grilled burger with mozzarella, pepperoni and fresh basil, and pasta dishes like salmon and broccoli linguini. Moroccan chicken kebabs, bangers and mash, lamb shank, and risotto cakes with grilled vegetables appear on the list of main courses. Home-made puddings include chocolate truffle cake with butterscotch sauce and cherry almond tart with apple sorbet. Lookout also for the choice of daily specials listed on the blackboard.

Well behaved children are most welcome.

Open from 10.30am till 3pm and from 6pm till 11pm (10.30am till 11pm Saturday; 10.30am till 10.30pm Sunday)

Telephone: (01590) 612324.

Beaulieu is situated on the B3054 between Lymington and Hythe. The Montagu Arms is right in the centre of the village.

Approx. distance of walk: $3\frac{1}{2}$ miles. O.S. Map No. 196 SU 386/023.

Parking is no problem. Apart from the forecourt there are two more large car parks at the rear of the hotel. Alternatively, there is a free public car park 250 yards away.

Beaulieu, famous for its abbey ruins and the National Motor Museum, has remained unspoilt, despite its many visitors. Our walk follows the Solent Way to the charming village of Bucklers Hard, a former naval shipbuilding yard in the 18th century (Nelson's fleet was built here), that nestles beside the picturesque Beaulieu river. The village has a fascinating little maritime museum which recalls this tradition and cottage displays recreate 18th-century life. Part of the return route winds through woodland along a delightful riverside path, otherwise the walk retraces the scenic outward journey. It is easy going underfoot and an ideal walk for the whole family.

1. Take the waymarked footpath (Solent Way) along the gravel track beside the hotel. Pass the rear car parks and continue to a stile beside a gate. Cross over and keep to the well waymarked and well walked route, with views across the Beaulieu river, past a small inlet and along the left-hand edge of a field. Eventually reach a house and a track and keep ahead, soon to bear right and then take the track left, signed Bucklers Hard.

2. Remain on this long and straight path through woodland. At a small car park, follow the gravel track right and shortly pass boatyards to reach the quay in Bucklers Hard. Having explored this attractive village, its museum and picturesque riverbank, return to the small car park on the edge of the village. Bear right onto a pleasant path that winds its way through the woodland, over tiny bridges and beside the tidal river. Eventually you will reach the main path close to the house passed on the outward leg. Turn right and retrace your steps back to Beaulieu and the hotel.

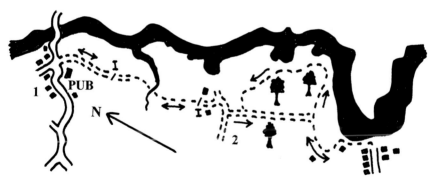

Key to Symbols

———— road	---------- track	---------- undefined path
∕ stile	bridge	⊢⊣ gate
⊣ ⊢ gap in hedge	cattle grid	

The Sun Inn, Bentworth

Hidden down a narrow lane on the edge of the village, the pretty flower-decked Sun dates from 1635 when it was two cottages. Today, it is a classic unspoilt country pub complete with heavy beams, board floors, high-backed antique settles, rustic scrubbed deal tables and two splendid fireplaces, one with a wood-burning stove and one with an open log fire, in the two traditional communicating rooms. A newer side room has a brick floor, an open fire and an array of hanging baskets, and maintains the unique traditional character of the pub. Various blacksmith's tools and attractive prints adorn the walls throughout. There are benches to the front and a beer garden to the side for fine weather drinking.

The Sun is a thriving free house offering an excellent range of real ales for beer connoisseurs. The choice of seven on handpump generally includes Cheriton Brewhouse Pots Ale, Courage Best, Ruddles Best, Badger Best, Ringwood Best, Ballards Best and regular guest brews like Timothy Taylors Landlord. The well stocked bar also has a good choice of malt whiskies.

Home-cooked bar food includes freshly-cut sandwiches, hearty soups (carrot and orange), ploughman's lunches, generously-filled jacket potatoes, chicken and ham pie, various pasta dishes and Cumberland sausage and mash. Lemon cream pie may feature on the interesting list of puddings.

The pub is open from 12 noon till 3pm and from 6pm till 11pm; all day Sunday from 12 noon till 10.30pm. Children are made very welcome.

Telephone: (01420) 562338.

Walk No. 3

Bentworth lies just off the A339 Alton to Basingstoke road, 4 miles north-west of Alton. From Alton take the second turning on the left for the pub; in the village follow the sign for Shalden/Alton.

Approx. distance of walk: 4½ miles. O.S. Map No. 185 SU 670/402.

There are two small car parks either side of the inn.

A pleasant rural ramble across farmland and through woodland, via well way-marked field paths and old droving tracks, in this unspoilt part of east Hampshire. Of note along the way is the interesting, early 13th-century church of St Mary which features a medieval font, with a charming pyramidal wooden cover dated 1605. Generally easy going underfoot but some of the tracks may be muddy in bad weather.

1. From the pub turn left down the lane. Where it curves sharp left at a junction, climb the stile on the right and walk round the left-hand edge of a field. Maintain direction along the edge of a second field to reach a stile in the field corner. Ignore stile and path on your right and keep ahead along the right-hand edge of the field to a stile. Cross a track and stile and turn right, following the yellow arrows around the field edge to a stile in the corner. Cross the tarmac drive and the stile opposite and walk along the left-hand edge of the field to a stile and field adjacent to the cricket ground. Keep ahead, climb a stile, pass through trees to a gravel drive and turn right to a road.

2. Turn right, cross the road and take the waymarked path across the stile on the left. Follow the path arrowed half-left across the field to a stile, then pass through a small plantation to another stile Climb the stile ahead, bear half-right across the field, ascending to a small wooden gate on the edge of woodland. Bear right on reaching the main track through the woods and keep left at a junction, following arrows to a stile on the woodland edge. Proceed straight on across a paddock (Gaston Grange to the left), pass through a gate and continue straight ahead across the centre of the field. Pass through a small plantation area on a defined track, then descend across the field to a stile onto a waymarked byway.

3. Turn right along the Oxdrove Way, following this wide track to a lane. Proceed ahead, soon to follow the 'Oxdrove' sign along the concrete driveway to Ashley Farm. Pass the house and outbuildings and gently climb the hedged green lane. Just before reaching Rushmoor Pond and a junction of byways, turn right to locate a stile in the hedge. Follow the defined path straight across the large field and pass through a belt of trees, bearing right to join a track leading downhill to a junction of tracks.

4. Turn left, then right just before a gate and follow the hedgerow uphill to a lane. Go through the gate opposite and bear diagonally left across a field and two paddocks via stiles to reach the small green in the village centre. Bear left to the lane and turn left, then right to reach the school and church. Walk through the churchyard, pass through the small gate and follow the tarmac path behind houses to the village lane. Cross over into a lane and follow it round back to the pub.

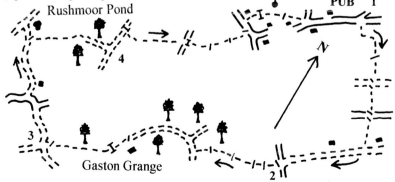

The Three Horseshoes, Bighton

Sadly these days more and more pubs are losing their identity, some are being turned into plastic restaurants serving fast food and gassy beer, whilst others compete for stars in gourmet guides. I'm happy to say this is not so with this delightful village local. A pub since 1612, it is owned by Gales, Hampshire's largest independent brewery.

There is a small comfortable lounge, originally the inn's living area, spotlessly clean with an open log fire and an unusual thatched canopy above. On either side are built-in settles and a wall display of police memorabilia. The cosy public bar is simply furnished with tables, chairs and wooden settles. It was originally two small bars, the reason for two fireplaces today, one of which has a warm log burning stove. On the wall is a collection of old gin traps and carpenter's tools. In summer you can make use of the peaceful lawned beer garden with picnic benches.

The pub offers three real ales, Butser Best Bitter, light, well flavoured and hoppy; the full-bodied HSB and dark mild. There is also a good selection of Gales country wines.

Bar snacks are available at lunchtime only (except Monday). You can choose from an assortment of sandwiches, various salads, ploughman's lunches and, during the winter months, a few hot dishes like home-made chilli and steak and kidney pie.

Children are welcome providing they are well behaved.

Open from 11am till 2.30pm and from 6pm till 11pm.

Telephone (01962) 732859.

Bighton is signposted off the B3046 just north of Alresford and from the B3047 (via Gundleton) close to the junction with the A31 Winchester to Alton road.

Approx. distance of walk: 4½ miles. O.S. Map No. 185 SU 614/344

Parking is available at the pub, in the lane by the telephone box or at the village hall.

A most enjoyable easy walk in this remote part of East Hampshire. Incorporating peaceful woodland, open farmland and an attractive long bridleway, it affords unspoilt country views and is an ideal family ramble, suitable for most weather conditions. Bighton is a pretty village with some splendid old houses.

1. Turn left from the inn and walk through the village, passing the turning for Ropley and a farm complex, to reach a driveway on your left. Go up the drive, pass a delightful cottage on your right, then on reaching a beautiful thatched cottage bear off left along a short drive, signed Flint Cottage (main drive to Bighton House veers right). At the cottage bear off right along a path into woodland. Keep left into a hazel copse and out into a field on the far side.

2. Follow the grass track to a waymarked stile and bear right, then left along a grass-centred track and soon follow it beside woods on your left, around the field edge to a junction of paths. Take the arrowed path left and shortly bear right, across the track and over a signed stile into a field. Turn right along the field edge, climb a double stile in the far corner and proceed along field perimeters via stiles to reach a metal gate and stile. Cross the stile and turn left along the wire fence, eventually climbing a stile beside a metal gate at the top of the rise onto a wide bridleway.

3. Turn left, keeping left where the track forks at Upper Lanham Farm and continue along this long bridleway until you reach a metalled lane by some cottages. Turn left and follow this peaceful narrow lane back down into Bighton. Keep left at the road junction and soon follow the main village road left back to the inn.

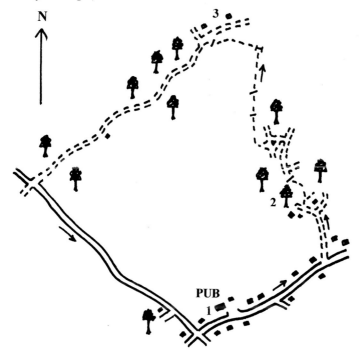

The Red Lion, Chalton

No book on Hampshire pubs would be complete without the delightful Red Lion, not least for the fact that it is the oldest pub in the county, dating back to 1147. It was first built to serve the stonemasons constructing the church opposite. The main bar has a low-beamed ceiling with heavy supporting timbers. Around the close-boarded walls are wooden settles with simple tables and chairs. At one end is a beautiful inglenook fireplace with its own built-in seat and warm open log fire; in front is an attractive, curved wooden settle and chairs around a circular table. The other low-beamed lounge bar is carpeted and also heated by a real open fire. A spacious side extension to the bar and a family dining are fairly recent additions and look out onto a neat lawned and terraced beer garden with glorious views to the Downs and Chalton Windmill.

The inn is owned by Gales Brewery of Horndean and offers their Butser Best Bitter, HSB, XXXXX - a dark sweet brew available in winter - and a regularly-changing guest ale. Expect a good choice of Gales country wines and over fifty malt whiskies.

Good home-cooked food is available daily. The choice ranges from lighter snacks like sandwiches and ploughman's lunches, to an interesting selection of daily specials such as sea bass marinated in lime and lemon, pork fillet en croute with chasseur sauce, roast guinea fowl with Calvados, and vegetarian dishes like roast peppers stuffed with mushrooms.

Open 11am till 3pm and 6pm till 11pm
Telephone: (01705) 592246

The small hamlet of Chalton is located a mile off the A3, about 5 miles south of Petersfield.

Approx. distance of walk: 3¾ miles. O.S. Map No. 197 SU 731/160.

The inn has its own car park at the side and rear.

An enjoyable scenic walk across farmland and through Queen Elizabeth Forest on well waymarked gravel tracks. Just off the route and well worth visiting is Butser Ancient Farm, a fascinating re-creation of an Iron Age farmhouse and field system (open daily March-November). Although mostly dry underfoot sections can be muddy during the winter.

1. Leave the inn and turn left, ignore the lane back to the A3 and take the narrow lane to the right of the small green. Walk straight across the Idsworth road and down the track (waymarked Staunton Way), passing farm buildings to enter a field on the right. Keep to the track as it bears left into another field and gently ascends along the field edge. Where it bears right, keep straight on across the field to a stile on the woodland fringe.

2. Turn right and keep to this defined track, following Staunton Way arrows, as it mean-ders through the forest, eventually rising to a crossing of tracks. Turn left and climb up and through the woods, then descend to reach a short gravel track on your left. Turn left and continue ahead on the grassy path (green-banded post), downhill to a T-junction of tracks on the woodland edge. Turn right, then where the track bears right (by a bench), keep ahead to a stile and bridleway. Turn left and follow it to a lane (Butser Ancient Farm right). Turn left along the lane for half a mile back to the inn.

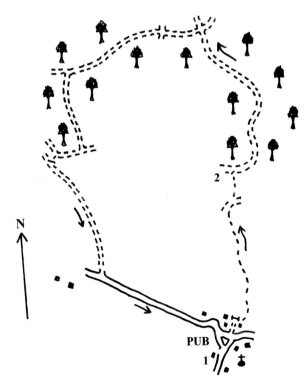

The Greyfriar Inn, Chawton

Little is known of the actual history of this friendly village local, only that it was once three separate cottages. It is a popular inn as it is sited opposite Jane Austen's house - the house itself is open daily from March to December (except Christmas); weekends only January and February. The inn has two inter-connecting bars with a wealth of old beams and standing timbers, and a separate family area with access to the attractive rear garden where summer barbecues are held.

The inn is a free house serving four real ales - Wadworth 6X, Greyfriar Bitter, Flowers Original and Boddingtons.

A varied bar menu offers good home-cooked food seven days a week with a traditional roast lunch on Sunday. Snacks include the usual sandwiches, plough-man's lunches, various filled jacket potatoes, salads and omelettes. Blackboard specials may include lobster thermidor, steak au poivre, liver, bacon and onions, wild rabbit stew, chicken Madras, braised oxtail and chilli.

The pub is open from 10am till 11pm Monday to Saturday and from 10am till 10.30pm on Sunday.

Children are welcome in the family area and dogs are permitted provided they are kept under control.

Telephone: (01420) 83841.

Chawton is well signed just off the A31, south of Alton.

Approx. distance of walk: 4¼ miles. O.S. Map No. 186 SU 709/377.

There is ample parking in two separate car parks to the right of the inn. Alternatively you can park safely in the village street.

Chawton, a pretty village, is probably best known for its association with Jane Austen who moved into Chawton Cottage in 1816. It was here she wrote Mansfield Park, Persuasion, Emma, Pride and Prejudice and Sense and Sensibility. This walk takes you through the village past Chawton House and then follows a peaceful bridleway to the small village of Upper Farringdon, returning via level farmland paths. It can be muddy in places in wet weather.

1. Turn left on leaving the inn and bear left at the bend along a dead-end lane, passing the school and Chawton House. Go up some steps at the end and turn left along the grassy verge of the very busy A32 (take great care here). In 200 yards take the arrowed footpath left over a stile and bear slightly right across a field and through a gate to join the wide bridleway leading to Upper Faringdon.

2. At the bottom continue ahead on the grassy track beside a play area and take the signed path left between hedges. Shortly, turn right along a track to the lane and turn left past the 13th-century church. Remain on the lane through the village until you reach a waymarked gravel track on your left. Take the first track on the right and pass through two gates, then keep ahead across a field, keeping close to the brook (on left). Go over a horsejump beside a gate and shortly cross the brook via a small bridge. Turn right alongside the brook, then at the end of the field climb the stile flanking a gate and turn left alongside the fence to a small gate.

3. Join a permissable path between wire fences that soon bears right towards buildings. At a waymarked junction of paths by a concrete track, turn left and keep close to the right-hand edge to a metal gate. Bear right across the field to a pair of stiles set in the hedge and maintain direction across three more fields and stiles towards a farm. Skirt round the farm via yellow-topped squeese-stiles through several fields to reach a stile on the edge of woodland. Follow the path down through the small wood to a stile, then bear left across a field to a further stile. Continue to a stile in the wall on the far side and take the narrow path back to the village street, turning left back to the inn

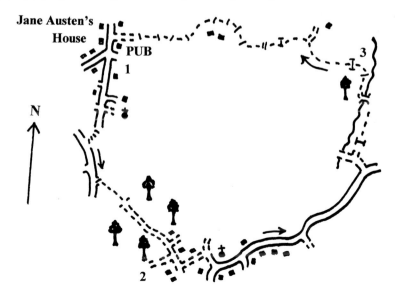

Jane Austen's House
PUB
1
N
2
3

Jane Austen's House, Chawton. Walk No. 6

Cheriton, Bridleway. Walk No. 7

The Flower Pots, Cheriton

Originally built as a farmhouse in the 1840's by the head gardener of nearby Avington House, the Flower Pots epitomises how a homely village inn should be. The unassuming brick exterior hides two welcoming and unspoilt bars. A traditional music-free atmosphere pervades in the larger rustic public bar, which is simply furnished with pine tables and benches, neatly laid out on a terracotta-tiled floor and fronting a brick fireplace and warming winter log fire. The glass-topped 30ft. well is an unusual feature. The cosy saloon bar has a drawing room feel with striped wallpaper, a comfortable sofa, wall settles, open fire and a large rug strewn over its wooden floor. An adjacent room has some easy chairs, numerous books and a television to keep children amused. Spacious lawned beer gardens to the front and rear of the pub have a mix of garden furniture.

Not only is the pub a free house, it brews its own beer in a purpose-built brewery across the car park. Its award-winning ales - Pots Ale, Cheriton Best, Diggers Gold and occasional brews like Beltane Ale, Chilli Beer and Turkey's Revenge - are tapped straight from the cask. Home-brewed cider is also available.

A short, value-for-money menu offers honest home-cooking and features beef stew, chilli, a range of jacket potatoes with various hearty fillings, excellent sandwiches, toasted and plain, and ploughman's lunches. A blackboard usually lists two or three hot dishes such as sweet and sour chicken and lamb and apricot casserole.

The inn has five well-equipped ensuite bedrooms in a converted barn annexe.

Children are allowed in the small children's room only and dogs are welcome in both bars.

Weekday opening times are from 11.30am till 2.30pm and 6pm till 11pm.

Telephone: (01962) 771318.

Walk No. 7

The picturesque village of Cheriton is situated on the B3046, 3 miles south of Alresford and the A31, and only a mile off the A272 at Hinton Ampner. The inn is located on the Beauworth road, west of the village centre.

Approx. distance of walk: 2¾ miles. O.S. Map No. 185 SU 582/284.

The inn has a good-sized car park.

This short, undemanding walk explores the pretty village of Cheriton, the Way-farer's Walk (WW) beside the youthful and idly flowing River Itchen and the surrounding bridleways that afford scenic views across this picturesque valley.

1. Turn right on leaving the inn, then at the T-junction in the village centre turn left, then right by the war memorial and village green. Pass the post office and turn right over the small bridge and right again into a cul-de-sac beside Cheriton School. On the left, beside the driveway to Martyrwell House, take the narrow, fenced path (WW) uphill out of the village to a stile. Bear right around the field edge to a further stile and crossing of paths.

2. Turn left, heading downhill to a lane (can be muddy at the bottom), and cross straight over, the narrow track soon merging with a wider track. Keep left and gently ascend to a junction of tracks (good views). Turn left and head downhill into the valley to the B3046. Cross over into a lane, signed Tichborne.

3. Cross the river bridge and take the waymarked footpath beside Cheriton Mill. Go through a gate and pass in front of a cottage to a stile. Follow the grassy path parallel with the river, crossing four stiles to reach a metalled lane on the edge of Cheriton. Cross the stile opposite and bear half-right across a field to a stile preceeding the play area and cricket ground. Follow the narrow path left along the fence and through a small cul-de-sac back to the inn.

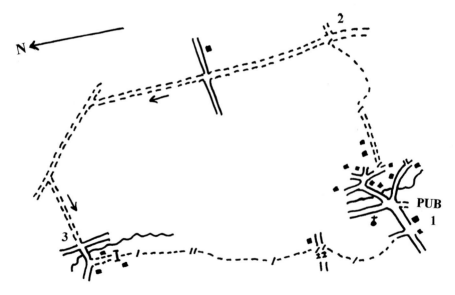

The sketch maps in this book are not necessarily to scale but have been drawn to show the maximum amount of detail.

The White Horse, Droxford

Located on the edge of the village, beside the A32, the White Horse is at least 500 years old. Formerly a courthouse - hangings took place outside - then a busy coaching inn on the route to the south coast, it is now an attractive hostelry sporting colourful flower baskets on its whitewashed facade and in the sheltered courtyard to the rear. There are rumours that a ghost, a lady dressed in grey crinoline, wanders through the upstairs accommodation - not for the faint-hearted if you stay here for bed and breakfast.

A complete mix of customers is usually to be found here, though bikers tend to congregate in the spartan public bar, while families and dining clientele favour the series of small cosy rooms, complete with low beams, alcoves and log fires, that make up the welcoming lounge bar.

Owned by Morland brewery, the inn offers a good choice of real ale, possibly including Ruddles Best, Greene King Abbot Ale, Flowers IPA, Morland Old Speckled Hen and IPA.

Reasonably priced bar food is served daily, the choice including snacks like hot crusty French sticks, sandwiches, salads and spicy Cumberland sausage. In the lounge bar blackboards list the choice of main meals. From smoked haunch of venison, crab paté, chilli and grilled sardines, the selection may extend to roast rib of beef, home-made chuck steak, mushroom and onion pie, chicken with couscous and peppers, fish pie and turbot with tomato and basil sauce. In season lookout for game dishes (pan-fried venison medallions with cranberry and wine sauce, pheasant, wild rabbit) from local shoots and suppliers.

Children are welcome in the family room and restaurant.

Accommodation is provided in three bedrooms (one ensuite).

Open 11am till 11pm (Sunday 12 noon till 10.30). Food is served from 12 noon till 2pm and from 7pm till 9.45pm Monday to Friday (12 noon till 9.45pm at weekends).

Telephone: (01489) 877490.

Walk No. 8

Droxford lies in the Meon Valley on the A32 between Fareham and Alton, 4 miles north of Wickham.

Approx. distance of walk: 3 miles. O.S. Map No. 185 SU 606182.

There is a small car park behind the inn; alternatively park just down the road near the church.

An enjoyable short stroll through the idyllic Meon Valley, initially following the idly flowing Meon river on the Wayfarer's Walk to the pleasant village of Soberton with its fine church, complete with a turreted perpendicular tower and Roman coffin. The return route gently ascends across farmland providing delightful downland and valley views. Droxford's mid 12th-century church is well worth closer inspection.

1. Leave the inn and turn right along the main road (taking great care) and keep right by village parking area towards the church. Follow Wayfarer's Walk (WW) markers into the churchyard and keep ahead, following path around edge of churchyard, then left through avenue of trees to a kissing-gate and a footbridge over the River Meon. Follow grassy path ahead, then follow WW marker right and walk parallel with the river to a stile. Continue through river meadow to the next stile, then bear slightly left across meadow to follow path along the edge of copse to a stile. Cross a meadow, heading towards a bridge and climb a stile on to the road.

2. Turn left, cross an old railway bridge and take the arrowed WW sign right across a stile. Bear diagonally right across field, soon to follow fence around churchyard to a swing-gate in the field corner. Turn right along lane, pass White Lion pub and turn

right through Soberton village. Just beyond telephone box take waymarked path left and soon join track through farmyard, eventually reaching a lane. Just before the lane climb the arrowed stile on your left and gently climb along the left-hand field edge to a gate. Maintain direction, soon to leave field edge to cross field to a stile beside a lane.

3. Keep ahead along wide track (Crookhorn Lane) which soon curves sharp right then left. In approximately 100 yards lookout for defined path on your left across a crop field (not waymarked), which eventually leads

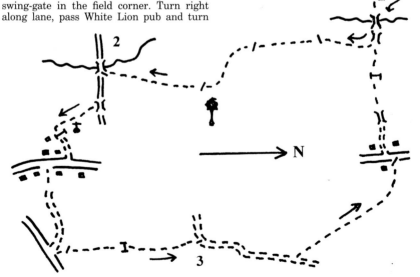

you to a stile and a lane. Turn left, then right down a bridleway, following track between properties and across an old railway bridge to reach a kissing-gate. Follow worn path back down to and across the River Meon. At the churchyard in Droxford, keep left of church on narrow path, then turn left at next gate away from churchyard. At a junction of path keep right uphill to the A32 and turn right back to the inn.

The River Meon. Walk No. 8

The Queen Inn, Dummer

I would think few people outside the village of Dummer had heard of the Queen Inn until the press made the pub their own for a time when Sarah Ferguson, whose family lived in the village, married Prince Andrew and became the Duchess of York; a subsequent party to celebrate the birth of their first baby was also well reported. It is an attractive pub dating from the 14th century, having one main bar with several cosy seating and dining areas. The whole interior is attractively furnished and warmed by a log fire in winter. To the rear of the pub there is a large garden and flower-decked patio for fine weather drinking.

Owned by Courage, the pub serves Courage Best and Directors Bitter, Marstons Pedigree and a regular guest ale such as Fuller's London Pride.

The inn offers an excellent menu: apart from the usual pub snacks - huge sandwiches and home-made country fare soup - there are hot beef and onion baps. All steaks are fresh Scotch Angus offered with a choice of home-made sauces. Fish dishes include fresh salmon and sea bass, while other menu choices may include chilli, deep-pan lasagne, seafood au gratin, Cajun chicken breast and rack of lamb with an apricot sauce. Several sweets include special sundaes and home-made puddings. Extensive wine list.

Opening times are from 11am till 3pm and from 5.30pm till 11pm.

Both children and dogs are welcome inside.

Telephone: (01256) 397367.

Picturesque Dummer is easily reached from the A33 and the M3 (junction 7), south-west of Basingstoke.

Approx. distance of walk: $5\frac{1}{2}$ miles. O.S. Map No 185 SU 588/462.

The inn has a small car park to the front plus there is limited parking along the road.

An easy walk along established tracks, including the Wayfarer's Walk, through Nutley Wood and along country lanes.

1. From the inn turn right, then bear round to the right at the junction opposite the church and turn left along the gravel track, signed Wayfarer's Walk, through a farm-yard. Keep ahead on merging with a con-crete farm road, then where this ends bear sharp left to follow the track round and down to a junction of tracks near a house. Turn right, then shortly right again along the tarmac drive leading to a cattle-grid and lane.

2. Turn left and follow the lane (can be busy) for nearly a mile and take the narrow lane on the left (just before a right-hand bend). On reaching the B3046 turn left and in 200 yards, just past the gates to Nutley Manor Farm, take the bridleway on the left, signed to Dummer.

3. Go up the track, through the gate and bear right past farm buildings to join a stoney track that gently climbs to a junction of ways. Keep ahead along the grassy track and soon enter Nutley Wood on a defined bridleway. On leaving the trees, bear right then left on a good track, downhill to a lane. Keep left and follow it back to Dummer church, turning right back to the inn.

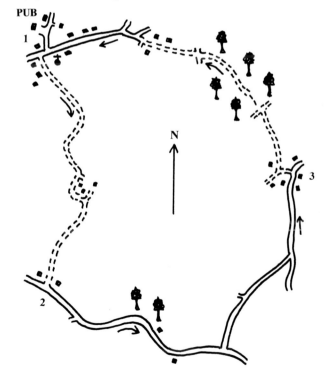

The sketch maps in this book are not necessarily to scale but have been drawn to show the maximum amount of detail.

The Hampshire Bowman, Dundridge

Throughout Hampshire there are a number of simple isolated country pubs, serving rural communities, that have changed little over the years. They are not smart but have a warmth and character sadly lacking in many modern-day pubs - the Hampshire Bowman is one of these. Tucked away in the small hamlet of Dundridge, in a peaceful spot overlooking open fields, it was originally a private Victorian house, built in 1862, before becoming an inn in 1897. From the front porch you enter directly into the bar, originally two rooms, at end there is a small servery and fireplace with a wood-burning stove; at the other is a lounge area with an open log fire. Furnishings consist of comfortable old chairs, wooden settles and an assortment of ancient tables, all laid out on the original brick floor. Around the walls are various old and interesting artefacts, pictures and even the old deeds relating to the property. Thankfully there are no electronic machines of any sort. At the back of the pub there is a large beer garden with children's play area, and picnic benches front and back.

The pub is a free house, dispensing ale in the traditional way straight from the barrel. The choice usually includes Archers Village and Golden, Ringwood Forty-niner and a guest ale.

A selection of traditional bar food is offered daily, except Monday and Sunday evenings, the choice ranging from snacks such as ploughman's lunches and sandwiches, to ham, egg and chips and sirloin steaks. There is usually a tasty home-made soup and a few daily specials on the blackboard to supplement to main menu.

Children are not allowed inside the pub; dogs are welcome.

Open 11am till 2.30pm (Monday 12 noon till 2pm; Saturday till 3pm) and from 6pm till 11pm

Telephone: (01489) 892940.

Dundridge, a remote hamlet, can be reached either from the A32 at Droxford or the B3035 just north of Bishop's Waltham.

Approx. distance of walk: 5¼ miles. O.S. Map No. 185 SU 578/185.

The pub has a good-sized car park.

An enjoyable country walk that incorporates established bridleways, woodland paths and a quiet country lane through the hamlet of Dean. Part of the ramble traces the Wayfarer's Walk, a long-distance path (70miles/112kms) linking Emsworth and Inkpen Beacon.

1. Turn left from the inn along the Upper Swanmore road and soon turn left again up the concrete drive towards Galley Down Farm. Pass between the house and barn and cross a stile into a field. Keeping fairly close to the right-hand hedge walk across paddocks via stiles, then ignore the stile on your right at the top of field, keeping to the edge of paddocks and cultivated fields (crossing five stiles) to reach a stile and track.

2. Turn left, then left again on reaching the lane, walking round until you reach the turning for Hazelholt Farm on the right. Keep to the main drive, past several buildings and through woodland to reach the B3035 (can be busy). Cross straight over and proceed across a field on a defined path towards woodland. Turn left along a bridle way (Wayfarer's Walk) at the woodland edge and follow it to a road. Turn right, then at a crossroads turn left (beware of fast traffic) and in half-a-mile take the arrowed bridleway on the left.

3. Keep to this wide track through woodland, then where it curves left at the end of the trees, keep ahead between fields (can be overgrown in summer). When you reach Franklin Farm on the left the bridleway merges with the gravel drive and bears right down to meet a lane. Turn left into the hamlet of Dean and take the first turning left, following the lane uphill to the main road. Go straight across onto the bridleway, following it through woodland and along the edge of a field to a lane. Turn right back to the inn.

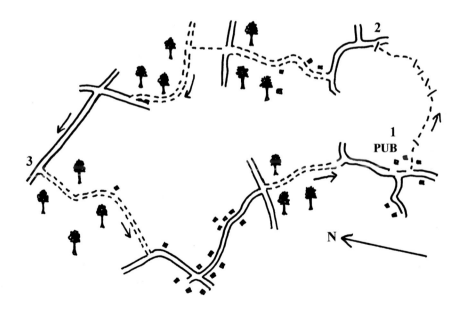

The sketch maps in this book are not necessarily to scale but have been drawn to show the maximum amount of detail.

The Farmers Home, Durley

At first sight the age of this lovely village inn can be deceptive, as it is not until you are inside that it becomes apparent. It dates back to 1747 (coincidentally the same year the Whitbread brewery was founded), and prior to then it was a slaughter house. Two inter-connecting bars and a cosy, recently extended dining area all have attractive brick or panelled walls and beamed ceilings, supported in one room by a couple of timber props. Each room has its own fireplace, the largest with a warm log fire, and a large collection of old artefacts, pictures, horse brasses, simple chairs, tables and wooden settle help create a warm and friendly atmosphere. At the back of the inn is a delightful beer garden and children's play area with an aviary and pet rabbits.

The pub is a free house offering four real ales - Bass, Wadworth 6X, Ringwood Best and Flowers Original.

Excellent food is available daily, all home-made using only the freshest of ingredients. You can choose from the regular bar snack menu or select one of the interesting dishes from the main menu. Hearty snacks range from jacket potatoes (salmon with mayonnaise), ploughman's platters, sandwiches (home-cooked beef), and mixed seafood platter. A typical meal may begin with green-lipped mussels in garlic butter, or country paté, followed by whole Dover sole, beef stroganoff, chicken in brandy and mushroom sauce, or a choice of steaks, including peppered fillet and mixed grill. Round off with banoffee pie or treacle sponge.

Both children and dogs are welcome inside.

Open from 11am till 3pm and from 6pm till 11pm Monday to Friday; 11am till 11pm Saturday; 12 noon till 10.30pm Sunday.

Telephone: (01489) 860457.

Durley is a small village signposted off the B3354 and B3035 north of Botley.

Approx. distance of walk: 2¾ miles. O.S. Map No. 185 and 196. SU 516/160.

The pub has a good-sized car park and it is just possible to park in the road to the front.

A short but delightful walk across farmland and along peaceful country lanes. Generally easy going but some parts can become very muddy underfoot during bad weather.

1. Turn right on leaving the inn and walk through the village until you come to a waymarked stile on the left (immediately opposite a junction). Proceed down to the bottom of the field and follow the short track up to a stile. Keep ahead across a field to a stile and gate, then follow the track uphill towards Hill Farm. Cross a further stile by a gate, then bear right passing red-brick houses and soon reach a lane.

2. Turn right, then in a few steps climb the stile in the hedge on the left and keep close to the right-hand hedge. Pass a house, cross a stile beside a gate and maintain direction over a field to a further gate. Follow the defined path across to a stile preceeding a hazel copse and keep to the path to a stile on the far side, then drop down to a lane. Turn right, pass Durley Mill and soon turn left into the drive of Durley Mill Farm.

3. Climb the stile on your right, enter a field and keep close to the left-hand edge until you reach a path on the left leading down to a stile. Enter woodland and bear right, follow the path through the edge of the wood to a stile and a lane. Turn left and soon take the next lane left, signed Durley. On reaching a junction turn left back to the inn.

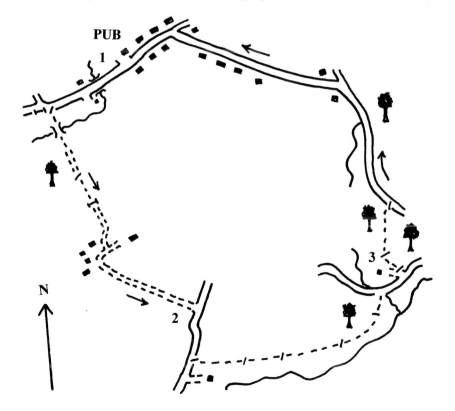

The George, East Meon

East Meon is a peaceful village nestling in the beautiful South Downs of East Hampshire. The George, originally a farmhouse built in the 17th century, is situated close to the church in the old part of the village. The original living area of the farmhouse is a delightful restaurant with a wealth of old beams and two large open fireplaces. The former cattle sheds are now two inter-connected rooms served by the same central bar.

The inn is a free house offering a good selection of real ales, possibly including Cheriton Brewhouse Pots Ale, Greene King IPA and Abbot Ale, Fuller's London Pride and Hall & Woodhouse Tanglefoot.

Good home-cooked pub food is served daily with the set lunch on Sundays proving very popular. Choose from the regular bar menu (sandwiches, salads, ploughman's lunches, filled jacket potatoes and various grills), or look to the blackboard for imaginative specials such as pheasant with cranberry confit, duck with citrus and juniper sauce, and venison with prune and red wine sauce. Vegetarian options may include red onion tarte tatin and wild mushroom risotto. Separate restaurant menu. Alfresco eating can be enjoyed on the front patio with views of the pretty church and village street, or on the sheltered rear terrace.

For walkers arriving back late cream teas are served in the bar during the afternoon.

Children and dogs are welcome inside, and overnight accommodation is available in small but comfortable bedrooms.

Open from 11am till 11pm (12 noon till 10.30pm Sunday).

Telephone: (01730) 823481.

East Meon is signposted from West Meon on the A32 Fareham to Alton road. Alternatively it can be reached from the A272 Winchester to Petersfield road.

Approx. distance of walk: 4 miles. O.S. Map No. 185 SU 680/222.

The inn has a car park to the rear, but you can also park safely in most of the village roads, or in the car park on the western edge of the village.

A lovely scenic walk through the picturesque Meon Valley. Although a little hilly in places, the farmland and woodland paths are generally easy going and suitable for the whole family.

1. Leave the inn and turn left towards the church. Go through the lych-gate and up past the church, following the signed footpath left. Ignore the stile on your right and eventually reach a stile and field. Keep close to the fence on the left and proceed to the stile on the far side. Maintain direction across another field to a stile in the hedge opposite. Keep ahead to a gravel drive to a house and bear left to the lane. Turn right and soon reach a waymarked stile by a gate on your left. Turn right along the grassy path on the field edge, climb a stile (beside gate) on the far side and continue ahead, down the field to a similar stile and gate at the bottom. Follow the defined path across the next field and stile opposite and bear slightly right over the next field to a stile in a hedge. Continue ahead keeping close to the hedge on your left, then go through a gate and follow the narrow path to a road.

2. Turn left, cross the River Meon and pass a brick and flint cottage, then turn right up Halnaker Lane (waymarked by-way). Ascend past a few houses into woodland. Where the track narrows keep left of the forest gate to follow a long track (can be muddy in winter) through the woodland fringe. After you leave the woods the hedged track continues between fields, eventually reaching a junction with the South Downs Way. Turn left and walk along the field edge towards Garston Dairy on the far side. Follow the path right, behind the wire fence, round the farm buildings to reach the concrete farm drive. Walk down the drive to the road; East Meon is visible to your left.

3. If you are feeling tired or it's ten minutes to closing time you can turn left back to the pub, otherwise turn right along the lane to the woodland and take the waymarked track on your left. Head uphill taking the right fork through the trees until you come to a gate at the top. Go through and, keeping close to the hedge on the left, walk across the field to a further gate. Go down a short track, cross a stile into a field and keep right downhill to the bottom of the field. Locate a gap in the hedge (footpath fingerpost) and continue ahead across the field, bearing left at the corner of the enclosed field. Walk straight ahead, go across the middle of the field, over the stile on the far side and through a car park to the road, Turn right, then right again at a small crossroads back to the inn.

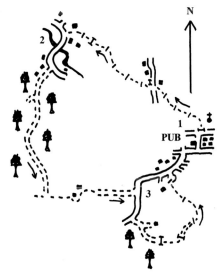

The sketch maps in this book are not necessarily to scale but have been drawn to show the maximum amount of detail.

31

The Chestnut Horse, Easton

Quietly situated near the Itchen this lovely atmospheric pub is well worth seeking out. The beamed bars are comfortable, warm and welcoming being heated by open log fires. One heavily-beamed rear dining room, dominated by a large open fireplace with a wood burning stove, is tastefully decorated in bottle green whilst the other similar in appearance also boasts a wood burning stove and is attractively furnished with an assortment of chairs, tables, pew seating and a large wall settle with lots of comfortable cushions.

The well stocked bar in this freehouse at present includes four real ales, London Pride, Draught Bass, The Chestnut Horse Special Bitter and Courage Best.

A wide range of food is served during the week from 12 noon till 2.30pm and 6.30pm till 9.30pm and all day Sunday starting with brunch at 10am. Traditional bar snacks which include home-made steak and kidney pudding, bangers and mash, a home-made curry and home-cooked ham and eggs are listed alongside home-made salmon fishcakes with a yoghurt, cucumber and mint sauce plus tempting appetisers such as hot garlic bread, avocado and warm bacon salad and deep-fried brie with fruit coulis. The evening blackboard menu might list starters such as cream of artichoke soup, mushrooms stuffed with garlic and Stilton, pork and Calvados paté and warm garlicky chicken liver, potato and bacon salad. Main dishes could range from chicken breast stuffed with wild mushrooms and bacon with balsamic, cranberry and sage sauce to slow roasted half-shoulder of English lamb with redcurrant and rosemary sauce, and roast duck breast with port and raspberry sauce. Fish dishes available on my visit included Scotch salmon and watercress en croute, cod fillet baked with a rarebit crust, and pan fried scallops with saffron sauce, wilted spinach and oyster mushrooms.

Families welcome, dogs on leads

Open from 11am till 3pm and 5.30pm till 11pm. Sunday all day 10am till 11pm

Telephone: (01962) 779257.

Village signed east of Winchester from the A31 and the B3047.

Approx. distance of walk: 3 miles. O.S. Map No. 185 SU 513/323.

The inn has a good sized car park at the rear and space in the lane.

A very enjoyable, mostly level, riverside walk in the pretty Itchen Valley. Apart from some winter mud the going is generally good underfoot, ideal for all the family, best though during the spring and summer.

1. Leave the pub turning left, go round the bend and take the first signed footpath on the left. Walk down the track to the small gate, through into the field and turn right then left making for the gate by the river. Cross the small bridge then the larger one over the Itchen leading to Martyr Worthy. Walk up the lane and turn left beside the church then join the narrow footpath leading to the field. Turn left down and round the field following the well signed path until you reach the lane.

2. Cross to the stile opposite and maintain direction to the stile following the path up towards the motorway bearing left to the underpass. Cross the stile into the field and keep straight ahead round and up beside the hedge out into the road.

3. Turn left past the dwelling and cross the stile into the field on the left. Bearing right keep to the well-beaten path, which drops down to a kissing gate. Turn left, cross the bridge and follow the attractive path ahead, which again crosses the river before reaching the lane. Go under the motorway turn immediately left and join the signed path which rises up across farm land eventually joining with a tarred lane. After passing St. Mary's church enter the village and turn right, then next left beside The Cricketers following the lane back to the pub.

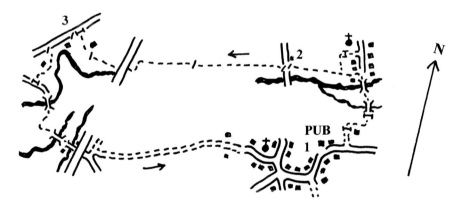

Views along the River Itchen. Walk No. 13

The Vine Inn, Hambledon

The historic village of Hambledon is famous, not least for being the birthplace of cricket. The first mention of Hambledon is in a charter of King Edgar, dated 956, granting the land at Chidden. In 1750 the world famous Hambledon Cricket Club was formed. It rapidly became the accepted authority and governing body of the game; it is therefore fitting that the village be referred to as 'The Cradle of Cricket'.

The Vine dates back to the 16th century, its age apparent once inside. Three communicating rooms in the main bar surround a large open fireplace; one of them, surprisingly, still has a genuine old well. The attractive beamed ceilings and walls, adorned with a wealth of artefacts, plates, pictures, clocks, brass, old copper and even a boar's head, help create the delightful atmosphere that prevails inside. There is also a good public bar and a lawned beer garden to the rear.

The well stocked bar of this free house offers no less than five real ales which may include Gales Butser Best Bitter and HSB, Charles Well's Bombardier and two regularly-changing guest beers.

Good bar food is available, much of it home-made and freshly prepared. Snacks include ploughman's lunches, filled baps and jacket potatoes and salads. Other dishes featured on the frequently-changing carte may include steak and kidney pie, home-made terrines and soups, curries and fisherman's pie. There is always a blackboard listing a choice of fresh fish dishes.

Both children and dogs are welcome inside the pub.

Open from 11.30am till 3pm and from 6pm till 11pm. No food Sunday evening or all day Monday.

Telephone: (01705) 632419.

Walk No. 14

Hambledon is situated on the B2150 between Droxford and Denmead. From the M27 (exit 10 or 11), take either the A32 or the road signed to Boarhunt - the village is well signposted. The inn is on the left in the main village street.

Approx, distance of walk: 4½ miles. O.S. Map No. 196 SU 645/150.

Park in the village hall car park next to the pub or in the village street.

A lovely walk, fairly easy going underfoot, with just the occasional muddy sections in winter. From the charming village of Hambledon, this ramble follows part of the Wayfarer's Walk, affording far-reaching views across the Solent to the Isle of Wight, returning via peaceful, well-waymarked paths and bridleways through woodland and across farmland.

1. From the inn turn left, walk along the main village street turning left opposite the post office into High Street. Enter the churchyard and keep left to pick up the Wayfarer's Walk markers (WW) and path on the left. Follow the narrow path down to a metal gate and head across a field to a further gate to enter a cul-de-sac. Go across the grassy area ahead to the road, turn right and, in a few yards, cross over to take the arrowed grassy footpath on your left. The path is fairly steep winding its way through woods to a stile at the top. Take the wide track ahead until it bears left by a field. Here, follow the narrow path on the right (WW markers on trees) which leads to a stile and large field.

2. Go across the field and bear right through a line of trees, crossing a stile on the far left-hand side into the next field. Bear slightly right on the defined path to a lane. Cross the stile opposite and follow the track across the field and bear left through the gap on the far side into the field ahead. Keep to the right-hand hedge to a stile flanking a gate. Leaving the Wayfarer's Walk, cross the stile and turn left along a good bridleway (can be muddy) beside woodland to a road.

3. Turn right, go down and around until you reach some cottages. Just beyond take the footpath left (not arrowed), a fairly long path that descends to meet a country lane.

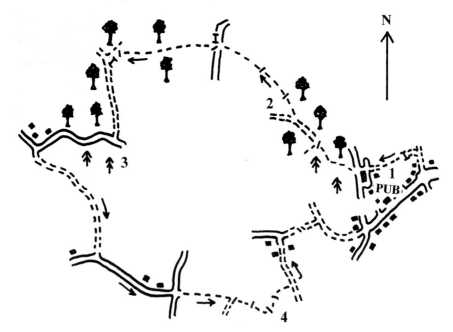

Turn left, walk up to the T-junction and go straight across through the gap into a field (waymarked). Proceed across, bearing left as you go, in the direction of the farmhouse. At the farm drive, go across the stile almost opposite, pass in front of the house to a stile and keep beside right-hand fence to a stile in the corner.

4. In a few yards cross the stile on your left (junction of paths) and follow path to a stile and paddock (yellow arrows). Keep right,

cross a further stile and walk along the field edge to a stile and enter woodland. At a wide track, turn left and keep ahead where it becomes metalled and descend to a lane. Turn left, then right along an arrowed footpath, following the grassy path alongside a garden wall to a stile. Proceed ahead, cross a second stile, then at a T-junction of paths, bear left downhill to the main road. Go straight across into West Street back to the inn.

Meon Valley view near Old Winchester Hill. Walk No. 12

Key to Symbols

══════ road	---------- track	---------- undefined path
⁄ stile	⟩⟨ bridge	⊢——⊣ gate
⊣ ⊢ gap in hedge	⊟ cattle grid	

The Prince of Wales, Hammer Vale

High up in a sunny position overlooking the pretty Hammer Vale sits the Prince of Wales inn and, although built as recently as 1926, it has a good atmosphere. One end has tables and chairs for those wishing to eat; the other is more sociable with just a couple of tables but plenty of standing room on the close-boarded floor and a warm wood-burning stove. It is the most easterly inn in the book actually bordering three counties - Hampshire, Surrey and West Sussex - and is owned by Gales, Hampshire's largest independent brewery.

Good real ale is still served traditionally, straight from the barrel. You can choose from Butser Best Bitter, HSB, XXXXX (in autumn and winter) and a guest ale.

Food is available daily; you can choose a dish from either the main printed menu or one of the daily specials. Good bar snacks include decent sandwiches (BLT, chicken with tikka mayonnaise), ploughman's lunches, burgers, filled jacket potatoes and pasta with Bolognaise sauce. Main meals feature New Zealand mussels in garlic butter, and whitebait among the starters, followed by home-made pies (chicken and ham, venison and mushroom) calves liver and bacon, mixed grill, red snapper with lemon and olive oil, or steak and kidney pudding. A roast lunch is served on Sunday and Friday night is fish and chips night. Vegetarian meals are generally available. The sweet selection includes home-made apple pie and treacly roly poly pudding.

Both children and dogs are welcome inside the pub.

Open from 11am till 3pm and from 6pm till 11pm (12 noon till 4pm and 7pm till 10.30pm Sunday).

Telephone: (01428) 652600.

From the A3 take the Liphook/Bramshott exit and head for Liphook, almost immediately turning left, signposted Hewshott; follow the narrow lane for two miles to the inn.

Approx. distance of walk: 2½ miles. O.S. Map No. 186 SU 868/327.

The inn has its own fair-sized car park.

The Hammer Vale is a lovely walking area with miles of public footpaths. This is a short, easy walk suitable for the whole family, however the paths can be very wet and muddy after prolonged rain and in winter. The first part of the walk is on country lanes; the second half along wooded bridleways. There is a beautiful walking area on the other side of the A3 around the lakes at Waggoners Wells owned by the National Trust.

1. From the pub turn right along the lane. Keep to this narrow road for nearly a mile until you reach Hewshott House. Take the unsigned bridleway on the left just before the driveway, following it downhill to cross the river and pass under the railway bridge. At a T-junction of bridleways, take the arrowed path left.

2. Continue ahead through woodland parallel with the railway line, ignoring the paths off to the right. When you reach a small gate go through into the field and proceed ahead to a stile. Keep straight ahead along the metalled driveway, following it out to the lane and turn left. Cross two bridges and keep to the lane as it bears left back to the inn.

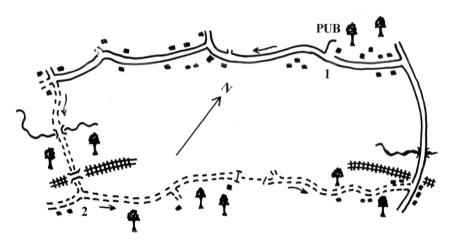

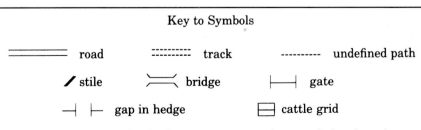

Key to Symbols

road   track   undefined path

stile   bridge   gate

gap in hedge   cattle grid

The sketch maps in this book are not necessarily to scale but have been drawn to show the maximum amount of detail.

The Hawkley Inn, Hawkley

Surrounded by beech-clad hills and attractive countryside, the friendly and unpretentious Hawkley Inn enjoys a peaceful position on the edge of the village. Accessed by narrow lanes, it is well off-the-beaten-track and has become an established watering hole among the walkers who tramp the Hangers Way between Queen Elizabeth Country Park and Alton. A relaxed atmosphere prevails in the open-up bar (no-smoking side room), with its individual decor and simple pine furnishings, and in the rear dining room. Posters and dried flowers adorn the bar and candles top tables in the evenings. There is a rustic collection of tables and chairs in the rear garden and several benches beneath the unusual front verandah.

The inn is noted for its well kept ales, the six regularly changing beers generally come from local brewers. A typical choice may include Cheriton Brewhouse Pots Ale, Ballards Best, Hopback Summer Lightning, Arundel Best, Oakhill Yeoman and Otter Ale.

In addition to decent real ale, the Hawkley attracts a good dining clientele. Two daily-changing blackboards lists the interesting range of food on offer. Apart from hearty snacks like generously-filled baguettes, several types of ploughman's lunches, filled baked potatoes and warming home-made soups (fish, ham and vegetable), diners can tuck into Tunisian fish tart, chicken liver terrine and ham and leek pancakes, followed by duck breast with peppercorn sauce, salmon fishcakes, paella, lamb tagine or salt cod and chirozo cassoulet. Round off a meal with summer pudding, fresh fruit crumble or orange and almond tart.

The inn is open from 12 noon till 2.30pm (3pm Saturday), and 6pm till 11pm, plus the usual Sunday hours. No food Sunday evenings. Children are welcome inside until 8pm. Regular live blues and folk music.

Telephone: (01730) 827205.

Hawkley is signposted off the B3006 between Alton and Liss, 2 miles north-west of Liss.

Approx. distance of walk: 4 miles. O.S. Map No. 186 SU 746/292.

Parking is limited to the lane outside the inn and beside the green.

A splendid rural ramble incorporating the Hangers Way, a 17 mile-long path that links Queen Elizabeth Country Park near Petersfield with Alton, following the beech-clad hillsides that run in a ridge across this area. On leaving this well waymarked route the walk follows bridleways, field paths and long-established green lanes, often affording rolling countryside views. Some of the sunken paths can be wet and muddy in winter.

1. Turn right on leaving the inn and keep left at the green (bear right to visit the interesting church with its unusual shaped tower). Bear left at the end of the green and soon turn right along a concrete drive, waymarked the Hangers Way. Follow the path to the right of garages, then along the edge of a field, gently uphill into woodland. Immediately turn right along the arrowed bridleway and follow this worn path close to the woodland fringe. At a fork of ways, keep right along the lower path (Hangers Way), then beyond fencing and field to your left, keep ahead down into a gully and up steps to a stile. Walk across the field to a stile in the far right-hand corner and follow the left-hand hedge to a stile and lane by a pond.

2. Turn left, pass Vann House, then take the Hangers Way right over a stile. Keep to the hedge on the left to a further stile and follow the worn path to two further stile and a lane. Turn right, ignore the HW sign immediately on the left, and follow the lane to a waymarked right of way on the right, just before a thatched cottage. Walk down this ancient green lane to a road and turn right. Shortly climb the stile on the left, cross the wooden bridge over a stream and walk through the copse to a stile. Bear left along a grassy track to a stile beside a gate and follow the defined path close to the fence and woodland on your right, eventually reaching a stile and a field.

3. Turn right along a grassy track leading to a metal gate. Go through and gradually climb a wide trackway (can be muddy). Pass a thatched cottage and barns, merge with the metalled drive, then take the arrowed path left, up the steep bank on the bend. Bear left around the field edge to a metal gate and the lane. Turn left, pass a house called Uplands then take the waymarked footpath right beside a gate and a large barn. Keep to this fenced path to a stile and a road junction. Cross straight over and follow the lane back to the pub and green.

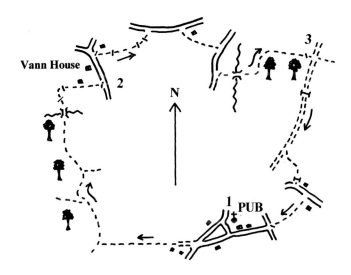

The High Corner Inn, Linwood

The High Corner has been for a number of years the ideal family pub. Tucked well away deep in the New Forest, it is an attractive inn draped with wisteria in summer and heated by an open fire in winter. The main building was built in the 1700s as a farm; now the old stables have been connected to the main inn with a linking building. The Stable Room is used for conferences and doubles as a very pleasant family room; the main bar is very cosy with beamed walls and ceilings with several rooms leading off. Outside is a large garden with picnic benches, a good children's play area and a barbecue area. If you feel energetic after your walk, the inn even has its own squash court.

Being a free house it offers three real ales on handpump, the choice may include Hampshire King Alfred Bitter, Wadworth 6X and Marston's Pedigree.

The inn is very popular for its food. From the set menu there is a choice of starters including soup, with main courses like steak and kidney pie with mushrooms, chicken Maryland, gammon and chips, fresh Avon trout, various omelettes and a mixed grill. There are, of course, the usual snacks such as ploughman's lunches and sandwiches, plus others like sausage platter and 'old smoky' - a fish pie with smoked haddock, tomato and cheese sauce, served with crusty bread. On Sundays there is a very popular all-day carvery.

Opening times are fairly flexible depending on the time of year but normally open all day during the summer from 11am till 11pm and in the winter from 11am till 2.30pm and from 7pm till 10.30pm (11pm Friday, 11am till 11pm Saturday).

For longer stays in this part of the Forest, the inn offers accommodation in six ensuite bedrooms.

Telephone: (01425) 473973

Linwood is signposted from the A338, Ringwood to Fordingbridge road. Continue through woodland onto the heath where the pub is signposted left, down a long gravel drive.

Approx. distance of walk: $3\frac{1}{4}$ miles. O.S. Map No. 195 SU 197/107.

The inn has ample parking, including two overspill car parks. Parking is not permitted in the gravel drive.

This most enjoyable New Forest ramble explores forest inclosures and open heathland tracks that afford far-reaching views across the Avon valley. It is an ideal family walk, the going is easy as the route follows wide gravel tracks, although during wet weather it can be muddy in places.

1. Turn left on leaving the inn and walk down the gravel drive, passing a few cottages. On nearing Dockens Water take the left fork and immediately bear right over the wooden bridge and follow the track round to the forest gate. Turn right before the gate, up the grassy path onto the heath (can be wet and boggy). On nearing the top take the path off to the right between an isolated group of pine trees and the wire fence of the inclosure. Continue round, turning right when you reach the wooden gate into Hasley Inclosure.

2. Go up the short track onto the main thoroughfare and turn right through this delightful mixed woodland. Go through the gate on the far side and continue ahead along a track across heathland. Shortly, turn right when you come to a distinct sandy path and follow it down to the stream and Splash Bridge at the bottom - a peaceful place to rest awhile. Proceed ahead into the woods, keeping close to the wire fence on the right. Cross the gravel forest track and follow the grassy path up to a further forest track and gate (numbered 89).

3. Go through the gate and keep to the track into the woods for some distance. Turn left on reaching a wide established path leading to a wooden gate. Go through, cross the forest lawn and the wooden bridge, then turn sharp left. Follow the narrow (often ill defined) grassy path uphill through scrub and trees. At the top, bear right to meet the gravel drive and turn right back to the inn.

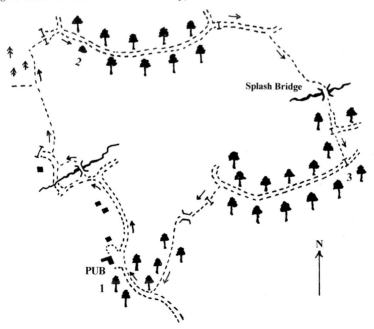

Splash Bridge

PUB

1

2

3

N

Splash Bridge. Walk No. 17

Minstead Church. Walk No. 18

The Trusty Servant, Minstead

Within the New Forest are many small villages, miles of beautiful walks and many lovely local pubs. Minstead is typical. The Trusty Servant is a simple village inn, rebuilt in 1901. The unusual sign outside depicts 'the trusty servant' who turns out to be a pig with a padlocked snout to illustrate his discretion and stag's feet to indicate his speed in running errands. He is also carrying a sword and shield in order to protect his master. The original picture and inscription hangs in Winchester College.

The pub consists of two bars; the Public Bar, complete with open log fire, where locals congregate and characters such as 'Cowboy George' can be seen; and the lounge bar where an enormous blackboard lists the 40 or so dishes available. Choices include an extensive fresh fish selection, good seasonal dishes, including local game, and traditional bar snacks like sandwiches, ploughman's lunches and salads. There is also a 45-cover restaurant - light and airy in daytime and candlelit in the evenings.

Owned by Whitbread the pub serves four real ales on handpump, including Ringwood Best, Wadworth 6X, Fuller's London Pride and Flowers Original. Diners will also find an extensive selection of wines.

Children are welcome inside; dogs in the public bar only.

The inn offers overnight accommodation in seven ensuite bedrooms.

Telephone: (01703) 812137.

Walk No. 18

Minstead is situated just over a mile from the A31 at the end of the M27 (it can only be reached from the west-bound carriageway). The village is also accessible from the A35 west of Lyndhurst and the A337 south of Cadnam.

Approx. distance of walk: 2½ miles. O.S. Map No. 195 SU 282/110.

Park in the car park beside the inn, by the green or the church.

A lovely walk, one of my favourites, through this historic New Forest village which boasts a splendid 12th-century church. One of only two listed in the Domesday Book, the church has some interesting box-pews, unusual galleries, and a 13th-century font; Sir Arthur Conan Doyle, the author of the Sherlock Holmes stories, is buried in the churchyard. The walk is easy going, along country lanes and woodland paths, ideal for the whole family.

1. Leave the inn and turn right up the lane to the church (well worth a visit). Take the signed footpath to the right of the churchyard; go through the gates and follow it round the field edge and into a small wood. Follow the path down to the gate at the bottom and turn right to reach a crossroads. Go straight across and up the lane beside the brook, signed to Furzey Gardens. At the end of the lane bear left, then left again up a gravel drive to pass Furzey Cottage (the gallery and cottage gardens are open 10am-5pm daily).

2. Go across the car park and down the waymarked path into the woods. In a few paces take the right fork, then having negotiated two walk-through stiles, cross a stepped board-walk and a bridge at the bottom. Go up the bank, climb a stile at the top into the field on the left and walk down to the right-hand corner. Cross the stile and follow the narrow fenced path to meet a lane. Go straight across, up and around the lane opposite to a T-junction. Turn left through the village to reach the crossroads by the ford you passed earlier. Retrace steps back through the wood to the church and inn.

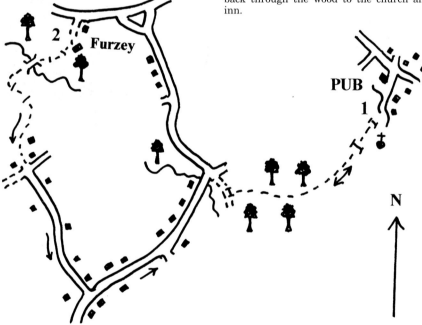

The sketch maps in this book are not necessarily to scale but have been drawn to show the maximum amount of detail.

The Isle of Wight

Old Town Hall, Newtown

To visit the I.O.W. is to step back in time. It very much reminds me of Dorset in the 60's peaceful roads with little traffic, it is for this reason I have included it within this book. I have picked just four of my favourite rambles which can easily be walked in a weekend. I stayed in very good bed & breakfast accommodation at Shalfleet but one can find lodgings almost everywhere.

The walks numbers 19-22 include a short coastal stroll, two walks onto the downs and a ramble which in part follows the bank of a brook. They vary in length from $1\frac{3}{4}$ to $4\frac{3}{4}$ miles.

The Hare and Hounds, Downend

Good vistas - variable walk.

Adjacent to Robin Hill Country Park, high up on the downs above the Arreton Valley, is the much extended and partly thatched Hare and Hounds. Formerly an unpretentious and unspoilt downland pub, owned by Burts Brewery, it is now a large, plushly refurbished family dining pub. The main open-plan bar area preserves many of the original beams, including the ancient 'Gallows Beam' which at over 22ft in length supports the roof of the old building. It once formed part of the gibbet which stood on Gallows Hill (adjacent to the inn), and last used at the execution of Michael Morey who was hanged for the murder of his grandson in 1735. The hangman kept a tally of his victims by cutting a notch in the beam every time it was used - the notches together with the date 1735 can still be seen. In a small glass case is a macabre human skull, said to be that of Michael Morey himself.

The inn is a free house and offers Ind Coope Burton Ale, Boddingtons and Morland Old Speckled Hen on handpump.

An extensive printed menu highlights a straightforward range of pub food. Crab soup, seafood fettucine and pan-fried herring roes appear on the list of starters, followed by steak and ale pie, grilled trout, lasagne, beer-battered cod and a choice of chargrills - farmhouse mixed grill, sirloin steak and turkey escalope with Dijonnaise sauce. Lighter snacks include filled jacket potatoes, ploughman's lunches, salad platters and a choice of freshly-cut sandwiches. Puddings range from sticky toffee pudding and hot apple pie to various cheesecakes and gateaux displayed at the food servery. Children are made very welcome, especially in the large rear dining area. Alfresco eating can be enjoyed on the rear terrace, with glorious views across the Country Park and along the downs.

The pub is open from 11am till 11pm and 12 noon till 10.30pm on Sunday. Telephone: (01983) 523446.

The Hare & Hounds is located adjacent to Robin Hill Country Park, high up on downland east of Newport. It is easily reached from either the A3054 Ryde road or the A3056 Shanklin road.

Approx. distance of walk: 4½ miles. O.S. Map No. 196 SZ 533/876.

The inn has a large car park to the side and rear.

A most enjoyable ramble that explores some of the scenic footpaths and bridleways that criss-cross the woods and farmland on this fine stretch of chalk downland in the heart of the island. Apart from glorious views, it takes in Arreton Manor, a superb Elizabethan mansion (open). Although a little hilly in places, the walk is mostly easy going but can be muddy during bad weather.

1. From the front of the inn turn left along the Brading road (it can be busy so take care). In about 200yds take the arrowed bridleway (N90) left down a gravel track, following it downhill to Combley Farm. Go through the gate, across the farmyard and through the gateway opposite. In a few yards take the track on the left and soon follow the arrowed path into a field, just before reaching some chalets. Turn left and follow the field edge, eventually reaching a small gate in the top corner. Walk up a narrow path (lined with an abundance of ferns and primroses in spring), turning left when you reach the drive at the top.

2. Turn left at the road and, taking great care, walk up past the entrance to Lynbottom Landfill Site. Shortly, turn right beside a gate (footpath 92) and climb the stile ahead into a field. Bearing half-left, walk up and across the field to a stile set in the far hedge. Cross the road and the stile opposite to follow the track alongside the left-hand hedge. Bear right and soon pass through the lower of two gates onto a wide bridleway. Turn left, following it downhill to the lane at the bottom. Cross the stile opposite (footpath AL5) and bear right across the field to a stile in the hedge, just behind an electricity pole.

3. Descend through a wood to meet a bridleway at the bottom and turn left. Pass a couple of houses, then keep left of a large green farm building to follow the bridleway steeply uphill. At the top, at a crossing of ways, take the waymarked bridleway left (it can be muddy after rain), walking down the ancient sunken path to the road. Turn right and immediately left along the Shanklin road into Arreton. Pass the entrance to Arreton Manor (open Easter to October, Monday to Fridays 10-6; Sunday 12-6) and the Country Craft Village, then just beyond the White Lion take the left on the left up to the church. Follow the footpath (A12) to the left of the church and soon ascend Arreton Down, keeping to the path along the right-hand edge of a field. Go up the steps, over the stile and bear left across the downs making for a stile in the far left top corner. Turn right along the road back to the inn.

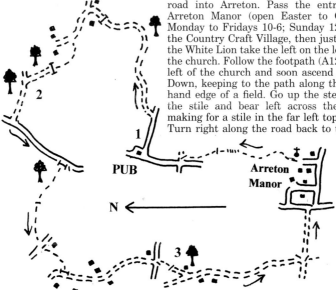

The Buddle Inn, Niton

Sitting high above St Catherine's Lighthouse, in the southernmost tip of the island, is the attractive Buddle Inn. There have been numerous suggestions about the origin of the unusual name - the most generally accepted being the old English word ' bothele', meaning the dwelling place. The exact age of the inn is unknown, but there is said to have been a cottage on the site around 1500. The present building was a farm and only granted its first licence in 1850 when it soon became known as a smuggler's haunt. The exterior remains much the same but alterations inside have seen the addition of a separate food servery and dining area. The original flagstone floor still exists together with an enormous old inglenook fireplace and some character tables and chairs. Outside there are picnic benches on the lawn and a barn to the side of the inn has been converted into a family dining area.

The inn is owned by Whitbread and offers several real ales, including Flowers Original, Greene King Abbot Ale, Fuggles Imperial, Bass, Boddingtons, Brakspear Bitter and a regularly-changing guest beer. Local wine and farm cider is also available from the bar.

Good food is served daily - you can choose from the printed lunch and evening menus or one of the daily specials listed on the blackboard. Meals include basket meals, ploughman's platters, home-cooked ham, egg and chips, cod and chips, steak and local crab or lobster salads. Specials may feature fresh local seafood and various curries and pies. Puddings range from apple pie and lemon sorbet to hot chocolate fudge cake and banana split.

Open from 11am till 11pm (Sunday 12 noon till 10.30pm).

Telephone: (01983) 730243.

Niton is situated on the A3055 between Ventnor and Chale. Take the turning for St Catherine's Lighthouse to reach the inn.

Approx. distance of walk: 1¾ miles. O.S. Map No. 196 SZ 504/758.

The inn has its own large car park opposite.

A short, but interesting, walk across National Trust land down to Knowles Farm and Watershoot Bay, returning along the coast path past St Catherine's Lighthouse. Certain parts are quite steep and it is a bracing walk in all but the calmest of weather conditions.

1. From the inn turn right along the village road and keep ahead at the sharp bend, signposted St Catherine's Lighthouse. Follow the drive to Knowle's Farm, keeping ahead through the yard to climb a stile by a gate. Keep to the grassy path as it gently descends to the pebbly beach at Watershoot Bay.

2. Turn left along the coast path and soon cross a stile over the wall close to the lighthouse. Follow the path to the other side, descend the wooden steps onto the cliff top and follow the path across open fields to a gate on the far side and enter a small caravan park. Keep to the left and follow the gravel access track out of the park and uphill. Go round a sharp right bend, then take the footpath left up a series of steep steps back to the village road and the inn opposite.

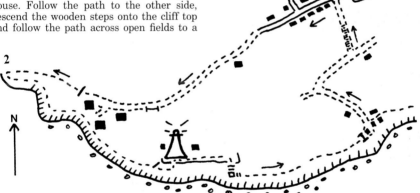

Inside The Buddle Inn, Niton

51

The New Inn, Shalfleet

Real pubs are getting harder to find these days but you do not have to look far to find this gem. Only four miles from the ferry at Yarmouth, the New Inn is on the Newport road in the pretty village centre of Shalfleet. It is a popular inn, and deservedly so, drawing people from all over the island to sample the lovely atmosphere and excellent seafood. Built in 1746, on the site of the old church-house, it remains uncommercialised and unhurried despite its popularity. There are two attractive bars and a lawned beer garden to the rear. The public bar has a fine original flagstone floor, scrubbed deal tables with wooden wall settles beside a large open stone fireplace with a warming log fire in winter; the other bar is more comfortably furnished with neat tables and chairs on a carpeted floor.

Real ale is still served traditionally, straight from the casks at the back of the bar. The choice may include Bass, Flowers Original and a guest beer.

The New Inn maintains its reputation for good food. Whilst snacks such as filled baguettes and ploughman's lunches are always available, the emphasis is on fresh seafood; mussels are a speciality - you can have them cooked in wine or with garlic. A blackboard in the bar lists all the daily specials: there is a choice of locally-caught fish such as cod, plaice, Dover sole and turbot; shellfish is much in evidence with local crab and lobster dishes. Besides fish there may be steak and ale pie, pork medallions with Dijon mustard and horseradish sauce, poacher's pie and chilli.

Children are welcome in the eating area of the bar.

Open all day (11am till 11pm) in the summer; 11am till 3pm and from 6pm till 11pm (11am till 11pm) in winter.

Telephone: (01983) 531314.

The inn is situated in the village on the A3054 between Yarmouth and Newport.

Approx distance of walk: 3½ miles. O.S. Map No. 196 SZ 415/893.

Either park in the inn's small rear car park or in the public car park 180yds along the lane.

Shalfleet is a delightful village just a stroll away from the old quay and Newtown Nature Reserve. Newtown, originally the island's capital, is today no more than a quiet creekside hamlet; only the splendid Town Hall (NT), built in the 17th century, is a lone reminder of this once important area. Both areas are worth further exploration. Our circular walk heads inland through Shalfleet and follows bridleways, quiet country lanes and farmland paths to Newbridge Mill, returning to Shalfleet church beside the Caul Bourne stream.

1. Cross the main road from the inn and walk down Church Lane opposite. Pass the church, then on reaching a T-junction turn left and pass the shop. Follow the lane round a few bends, then take the signed footpath on the right (S15 Ningwood). Go through woodland to a stile, then bear right across the field to another stile and bear diagonally left across to a gate and stile in the field corner. Go out into the lane and turn left.

2. In a short distance take the arrowed bridleway right (S16 Brook), and follow this across an old disused railway line, eventually reaching a road. Go straight across, up Dodpits Lane opposite, then turn left down the concrete driveway to Eade's Farm (bridleway S22). Pass the farm buildings, then at the bottom take footpath S22 on the right into the field. Keep close to the left-hand hedge and walk round until you are level with a thatched cottage on the left. From here go straight across the field and pass through an opening in the hedge on the

far side. The path winds through a small thicket, crosses a stream and climbs steps up a bank to reach a junction of paths. Turn left to a stile by a gate and turn left along the road.

3. As you round the bend, ignore the lane on the right, but climb the stile just beyond (footpath S35), and follow the well trodden path across the field to a stile beside a gate into a lane. Keep straight ahead, pass a farm and cottages onto a track, then cross a stile beside a gate and continue straight on where the track bends sharp left. Cross a further stile (footpath 17) on the right and follow the well defined path across the field down to the stream.

4. Climb a stile into the adjoining field and follow the course of the Caul Bourne via the occasional bridge and stile, eventually reaching a small green beyond the sewage works. Bear slightly left to join a narrow grassy path leading out to the lane opposite the church and turn right back to the inn.

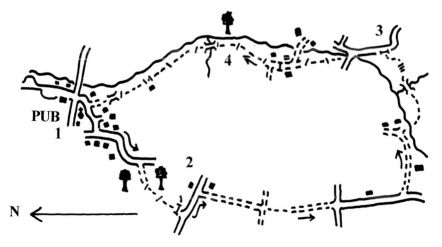

53

The Crown Inn, Shorwell

One of the loveliest pubs on the island, The Crown nestles beside a stream, opposite the church in the pretty village of Shorwell. It is an old inn, dating back to the 1600s and in its time has been a staging post for coaches and, more secretively, a quiet retreat for smugglers. Today it is a very pleasant place to enjoy a meal or just sit beside the trout stream, with a drink, watching the antics of ducks and doves. Two beautifully-kept bars have panelled walls, low-beamed ceilings and open log fires. The comfortable furnishings are a pleasant assortment of old tables, individual chairs and wooden wall settles - the larger bar has a lovely Jacobean oak dresser and there is a separate family dining area.

A Whitbread house, the Crown serves Wadworth 6X, Boddingtons, Hall & Woodhouse Tanglefoot and Flowers Original, as well as an extensive wine list, favouring New World wines.

The inn is well known locally for its excellent home-cooked food. The extensive bar menu (scampi, lasagne, burgers, salads, ploughman's lunches, pizza's, char-grilled steaks) is enhanced by good blackboard specials such as lamb casserole, fish pie, steak and kidney pie, salmon with watercress sauce, sea bream with crab sauce and crisp duck breast with black cherries. Vegetarians dishes may include nut roast with provencal sauce, and vegetable curry. Puddings include home-made fruit crumble and treacle tart.

Families are made very welcome; children have their own menu.

Open all day (10.30am till 11pm, from 11.30am Sunday) in the summer. Winter hours are 10.30am till 3.30pm and from 6pm till 11pm. Food is available from 12 noon till 10pm during the summer months.

Telephone: (01983) 740293.

The inn is situated in the heart of the village on the B3399 between Newport and Chale, 5 miles south-west of Newport.

Approx. distance of walk: 4¾ miles. O.S. Map No. 196 SZ 457/830.

Park beside the inn or in the large car park to the rear.

A delightful scenic walk, fairly long but mostly dry and easy going underfoot. The first half of the walk is level as it passes through the grounds of Wolverton Manor, a fine Elizabethan mansion (not open), to the historic 18th-century Yafford Mill and Farm Park; the second half steeply ascends Limerstone Down, the strenuous climb is rewarded with glorious views across the island. The route back to the inn follows the Worsley Trail and passes through the old part of Shorwell.

1. Leave the inn and turn right along the B3399 towards Brighstone. Pass several dwellings, then on the edge of the village take the arrowed footpath (SW3) on the left. Cross the stile and go straight across the field to another stile beside a gate. Turn right along the field edge, climb a stile and bear diagonally left across the field to a stile at the bottom. Go over and follow the narrow path over the brook and through Troopers Wood via a board walk.

2. At a house bear right, go across the stream, bear right again and pass through the gate on the left, up through the farm with Wolverton Manor to your left. At the lane turn right and continue walking until you reach the lane on the right, signed Yafford Mill. Pass the Mill and Farm Park (open daily 10-6), keeping to the lane between animal enclosures. At a T-junction turn right, then left at the next junction, soon to reach the B3399 at Limerstone.

3. Turn left, then almost immediately right onto a waymarked bridleway just past the farm. Follow the good track to the top, pass through the wooden gate and bear left, keeping to the right of the outcrop on an ill defined path/sheep track to reach two gates. Go through the one on the right and follow the left-hand field edge uphill to a small wooden gate at the top. Proceed ahead on the chalky track to the top of Limerstone Down and turn right along the waymarked Worsley Trail.

4. Keep to this long, established ridge track for some distance, passing through a few gates, eventually reaching the B3323. Take the link path on your right parallel with road, downhill through woodland, eventually reaching a stile onto Northcourt Farm's access road. Turn left, then right in a few paces along the B-road through Shorwell back to the inn.

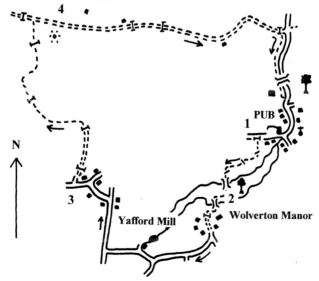

The Red Lion, Mortimer West End

Mortimer West End is a small village close to Silchester, where a Roman settlement flourished after the conquest of AD43. The church of St Mary the Virgin dates from the 12th century and stands on the site of two Roman temples; the north aisle is known as 'Mortimers Hole' because folk from Mortimer West End were allowed to worship there until their own parish church was opened. Three hundred metres to the west in the middle of the Roman town, hidden under the turf, is the earliest known urban church north of the Alps.

Situated overlooking green fields, the Red Lion is a welcoming country pub dating from 1575. There is one attractive carpeted bar and a separate dining area. The ceilings are heavily beamed with more timber and part-wood panelling on the bare brick walls; at either end are large open fireplaces, one with a log fire in winter. To the front there are seats on a sunny, flower-filled and sheltered terrace and, to the rear, further benches for fine weather drinking.

The Red Lion is owned by Hall & Woodhouse and offers five well-kept real ales, including Badger Best, Dorset IPA, Tanglefoot and beers brewed at the Gribble Inn, perhaps Reg's Tipple and Oving Bitter.

The main emphasis of this lovely pub must be the largely home-made food. There are the usual snacks such as ploughman's lunches, salads, filled baguettes and jacket potatoes, and open sandwiches. Main menu dishes range from tipsy mussels, wild boar and apple sausages, poacher's casserole, ham, egg and chips and cod and chips, to tuna steak and salsa, salmon hollandaise and Mediterranean pasta bake. Daily specials may include vegetable cobbler, steak and red wine pie and chicken korma.

Children are very welcome; there is a good play area in the rear garden.

Open from 11am till 11pm (12 noon till 10.30pm Sunday).

Telephone: (01734) 700169.

Mortimer West End is a small village in the most northerly tip of Hampshire, about 5 miles north of Basingstoke. Take the A340 Tadley road from Basingstoke and at Pamber End follow signs for Bramley, then Silchester to reach the village.

Approx. distance of walk: 4 miles. O.S. Map No. 175 SU 633/635.

The inn has a large car park.

A very interesting and most enjoyable walk in this delightful part of northern Hampshire. It is an easy walk, mostly dry underfoot with just a few muddy areas in winter. The first half of the walk takes you through the lovely wooded Benyon's Inclosure and across fishing lakes; the second half explores the unexcavated Roman town of Calleva. Sections of the perimeter wall are still standing and you also pass beside the restored amphitheatre.

1. Leave the inn and turn right. Just beyond the church cross over and climb the stile beside the drive to The Old School House. Follow the path down through the woods, cross a wooden walkway and bear left over the plank bridge and head back up into the woods, keeping close to the field on the left. On reaching a track turn right and shortly bear left down a short path to meet a wider gravel track and keep left. Go across the causeway between the lakes and bear right at the junction, following the track up into woodland. At a crossing of tracks (information board), turn left and eventually reach a stile and turn left along the road.

2. In a short distance turn right, signposted Little London, and bear immediately left down Bramley Road, turning left again onto the waymarked bridleway just beyond Calleva Museum. Follow the track to a stile, then continue ahead on the path to a small gate and the perimeter bank of Calleva. Turn left, then keep to the wide path across the centre of the walled town, bearing right on the far side through a small gate to reach the 12th-century church.

3. Go through the churchyard, out into the lane and turn left. At a sharp left-hand bend go through the small gate ahead to view the amphitheatre. Keep straight ahead at the bend down a track, soon to negotiate the squeeze-stile on the left into a field and walk towards the electricity pylon. Climb the stile in the hedge, go up the bank and the field ahead to a further stile. Turn left, passing under the pylon and round the field edge to a stile beside an oak.

4. Proceed ahead across the field to another stile, then bear slightly right towards two gates. Pass through the one on the right and turn left along the field edge, keeping right by a gate (yellow arrow) to a stile in the field corner. Turn left along the track, crossing the stile ahead where the track bears left towards barns. Keep to the field edge to a stile and the road. Turn right and take the arrowed byway right, opposite the Roman Town Car Park, following it to a road. Turn right back up the hill to the inn.

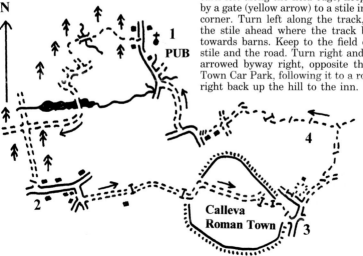

The Bush, Ovington

Hampshire is indeed fortunate having so many lovely unspoilt country inns like the Bush, an unspoilt 17th-century rose-covered cottage. Tucked away down a leafy lane, close to the River Itchen, it is hard to imagine that you are but minutes from the busy A31. Inside the inn are three cosy and atmospheric rooms served by the same bar. Each has its own fireplace with a warm fire in winter, and all around the dark walls are a wealth of old artefacts, brass and copper items, clocks, pictures, even an encased stuffed fish and enormous old bellows. The furnishings are a simple collection of elm tables, comfortable cushioned chairs and high-backed settles. A particular attraction in the summer is the delightful front garden and the short stroll along the adjacent path to a bridge over the Itchen.

Now owned by the Wadworth brewery it serves 6X, Henry's IPA, Farmers Glory and Hall & Woodhouse Tanglefoot on handpump.

Good bar food ranges from freshly-cut sandwiches, home-made soups (French onion), ploughman's lunches and starters like duck paté and baked avocado with prawns. Main dishes may include seafood tagliatelle, ratatouille au gratin, steak and ale pie and coriander chicken, followed by a selection of home-made puddings such as bread-and-butter pudding and spotted dick. Good selection of wines by the bottle and glass.

Children are welcome in the family dining area; dogs are also allowed inside. Open from 11am till 2.30pm and from 6pm till 11pm. Usual Sunday hours. Telephone: (01962) 732764.

January 15th 00: Pleasant summer walk by river and thigh woods with a long road walk 1 mile+ in the middle. Quite tiring towards the end - muddy this time of year. 2hrs first stop at church in Avington.

Ovington is signposted off the A31 between Winchester and Alresford. The Bush is located at the bottom of the village, close to the river.

Approx. distance of walk: 5¼ miles. O.S. Map No. 185 SU 561/318.

Park either in the inn's own car park or in the lane (limited space).

A fairly long, but interesting walk which twice crosses the beautiful River Itchen. It explores the tranquil village of Avington with its impressive Georgian church and follows a variety of paths across river meadows, open farmland, through peaceful woods (can be muddy) and along quiet country lanes. Much of the early part of the walk follows the Itchen Way, a well-waymarked route that follows the river from its source near Cheriton to Southampton where it enters The Solent.

1. Go down the footpath on the left beside the inn and cross the wooden bridge over the Itchen. Follow the gravel path left beside the river and soon cross a further bridge on the right to follow a lane up to the B3047 in Itchen Stoke. Turn left, taking great care as this is a busy road, and shortly turn left onto a gravel track (waymarked) just past River's Keep Cottage. Cross stiles flanking two gates and proceed across river meadow, via old stone bridge, to a bridge across the Itchen.

2. Bear right, then left over another bridge, following the path until you come to a stile on the right. Keep to the right-hand edge of a field to a stile, then bear diagonally left across a further field (large house right) and go through two kissing-gates. Bear right parallel with lane through field to further kissing-gate and turn right along lane passing Yavington Farm. Shortly, climb the arrowed stile on your left and bear right up the field to a stile and turn left. Take the arrowed path right leading to and through a clump of trees and soon follow wide path beside a golf course to reach the car park and gravel drive.

3. Walk down to the lane, passing through the kissing-gate on the left to follow narrow path parallel with the lane to a further gate and enter Avington, passing the unspoilt Georgian church which dates from 1770. Keep to the lane for just over a mile to Avington Manor Farm. Just past the farm take the arrowed bridleway left through a gate. Shortly, go through a further gate and gently ascend into Hampage Wood.

4. At the top of the bridleway, at a junction of paths just before Hampage Farm, take the small path on the left just to the right of a wire fence (do not go along the wide forest track). The path keeps close to the woodland fringe, winding its way (can be overgrown in summer and muddy in winter) down to a lane. Turn right, following the lane to a T-junction and turn left downhill back to the inn.

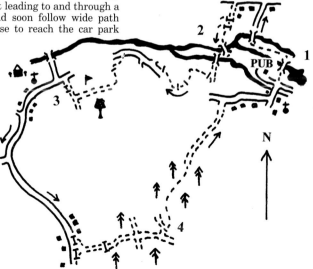

The Ship Inn, Owslebury

The Ship Inn, originally called the Britannia, dates back to 1681 and was used as recently as 1900 for the customary Court of Marwell Manor. It was once thatched but is now tiled and the tiled and rendered facade sports some splendid summer hanging baskets. There are two attractive bars; the Crow's Nest is the original bar and has a lovely atmosphere, complete with a wealth of beams, old ship's timbers serving as wall and beam props, and a fine fireplace with open log fire in winter. A rear and side extension houses the Mess Deck bar which is similarly furnished with local pictures and prints decorating the walls. The extensive gardens feature a marquee covered patio, a children's play area, pet's corner, summer Sunday barbecues, and petanque pistes. Look out for the winter jazz and quizz nights.

The inn is owned by Marston's and the well stocked bar includes Marston's Pedigree, Best and Head Brewer's Choice Ale, Bateman's Mild and a guest ale, plus a global wine list.

Traditional home-cooked meals are served daily, the choice ranging from good snacks like soups, sandwiches, ploughman's lunches and filled jacket potatoes, to an extensive selection of 15 daily specials such as moules, chicken balti, Irish stew, fillet steak with tarragon and cream, guinea fowl with mango and brandy, bacon and basil pasta, stuffed lamb's hearts, and salmon en croute.

Children are welcome in the Mess Deck Bar; dogs are also allowed inside.

Open from 11am till 3pm and from 6pm till 11pm (Sunday 12 noon till 10.30pm).

Telephone: (01962) 777358.

Owslebury is a peaceful downland village situated a short drive from the M3, south-east of Winchester. Approaching from the north, either take the signed lane off the A272 or leave the M3 (junction 11) towards Twyford (B3335) and follow village signs right in a couple of miles. From the south turn off the B2177 between Fisher's Pond and Bishop's Waltham.

Approx. distance of walk: 3½ miles. O.S Map No 185 SU 234/512.

The inn has its own car park and there is space to the front in a small crescent.

An easy walk through delightful countryside on well-established paths and tracks. Although it can be very muddy, especially in winter, it is an ideal family walk as it passes through woodland beside Marwell Zoological Park, a popular diversion along the way.

1. Turn right from the inn and in a few yards bear off left along a drive (signed Longfield). Disregard the arrowed bridleway right, then just before reaching the entrance to the house take the narrow tree-lined bridleway on the left; it is a lovely path edged with bluebells, quite long and can be muddy. On reaching double metal gates follow the path left (blue arrow) and skirt bluebell woods on your left, then cross a gravel track to enter woods, keeping left at a fork of paths. At the top of the rise (Marwell Zoo car parks left and right), cross the track and keep ahead along the often wet and muddy bridleway, eventually reaching the entrance to the zoo.

2. Cross the access road and follow signed bridleway through a narrow strip of woodland. Keep left beside a road, then almost immediately bear left (fingerpost) across a small area of open grassland and back into the woods. Keep close to the perimeter, at one point crossing a track back into the woods on the other side. On reaching a wire fence bordering a field, follow the path left and soon pass alongside enclosures with views of Marwell Hall.

3. Just before reaching a road follow the bridleway left beside enclosures, parallel with the road and eventually join the road. Just before reaching Whaddon Farm go up the short track (waymarked) on the right. On entering a field keep straight ahead alongside the hedge on the left. At the end of the hedge/trees bear diagonally left to a gate in the top corner of the large field. Proceed up the path, then track until you reach the church at the top. Go left up the steps and walk through the churchyard to the village lane and turn left back to the pub.

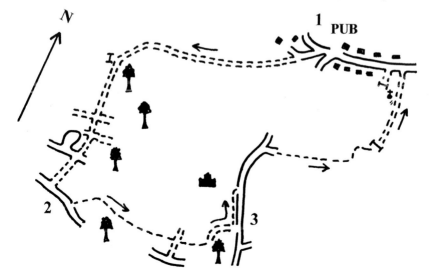

The Chequers Inn, Pennington

The Chequers, an unspoilt creeper-covered inn close to the sea and located in a peaceful rural lane, dates originally from the 16th century and was once the local salt exchange. It is a charmingly simple yet stylish inn bursting with character and a real favourite among the local yachting fraternity. The welcoming interior is simply furnished with comfortable chairs, various old tables and wall pews on the part-tiled and part-boarded floor, and is heated in winter with an efficient wood-burning stove. For alfresco drinking you will find a courtyard with picnic benches, and a neat walled garden with terrace.

It is a free house offering four real ales, including Wadworth 6X, Bass, Fuller's London Pride and a changing guest beer.

Good food is available both lunchtimes and evenings, the menu being chalked on the blackboard in the main bar. There are the usual pub favourites like jacket potatoes, ploughman's lunches, filled French sticks and home-made soup. Seafood naturally features strongly, including local crab and lobsters and excellent fresh local fish such as whole plaice, lemon sole and trout. In winter the menu highlights local game. Other dishes include rack of lamb, seafood lasagne, steaks, various pasta dishes and a selection of home-made puddings. Separate restaurant with a comprehensive à la carte menu.

Dogs are allowed inside, but not in the evening at weekends. Children are welcome away from the bar and in the restaurant.

Open from 11am till 3pm and from 6pm till 11pm (Saturday 11am till 11pm; Sunday 12 noon till 10.30pm).

Telephone: (01590) 673415.

From the A337 at Pennington (just west of Lymington), turn left along Ridgeway Lane; the inn is on the right.

Approx. distance of walk: 4½ miles. O.S. Map No. 196 SU 322/936.

Park at the front of the inn.

An enjoyable walk along field paths, quiet country lanes, wide gravel tracks and a bracing section of coastal path (Solent Way), which affords good views across to the Isle of Wight and Hurst Castle, as well as the opportunity to see a wide variety of birdlife on the inland pools and marshes.

1. Turn right on leaving the inn, then immediately right again along a 'private road' (the footpath is signed). Just before reaching the entrance to Pennington House, climb the waymarked stile on the right and follow the narrow path up to a second stile. Enter a field and in a few paces cross the stile in the hedge on the right. Turn left alongside the hedge to a further stile and keep ahead along the left-hand edge of the next field to reach a stile and a lane.

2. Turn left and in a short distance take the arrowed path right beside a metal gate. Follow the metalled track to a gate, then join a grassy track that eventually leads to a stile and access road to the council tip on your left. Cross the stile opposite and turn left along the gravel track. Remain on this long track past fields and old quarries, eventually crossing a stile beside a gate onto a lane.

3. Turn right and soon enter Keyhaven. As you reach the car park beside the sea wall, take the signed footpath on the left (Solent Way) through a gate. Follow this scenic coastal path along the length of the shoreline, past Pennington Marshes and historic salt beds. When you reach a small jetty turn left, go through a gate and head inland along a gravel track. Pass through two more gates and turn right on reaching a lane. Shortly, turn right along a signed footpath, pass a few houses and join a country lane. Follow it round back to the inn.

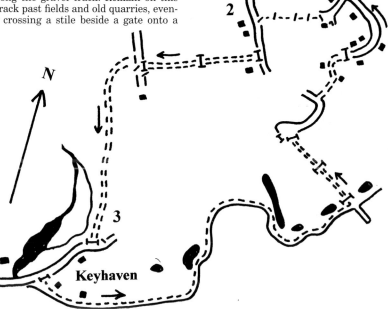

The sketch maps in this book are not necessarily to scale but have been drawn to show the maximum amount of detail.

The Fleur-de-Lys Inn, Pilley

Sometimes during my walks I come across an inn I've not visited before, but it is rare to find an inn as old and as charming as the Fleur-de-Lys, that I have to admit was previously unknown to me. In the entrance passageway is a list of all the landlords since 1498 although beer is believed to have been sold here since 1096. Originally the inn was a pair of forester's cottages; the tree roots and fireplace opening (an old New Forest Rights tradition) can still be seen in the stone-flagged entrance passage. The inn was described in Sir Arthur Conan Doyle's book 'The White Company', and the two bars are named after characters from the book 'The Children of the New Forest' which was written in the locality.

The lounge is very attractive with a heavy beamed ceiling and walls covered with old artefacts, copper and antique brass items. At one end is a beautiful inglenook fireplace where, until a few years ago, ham was still smoked in the chimney. There is also a small family dining area and a pretty garden to the rear.

Real ale is still served in the traditional way, straight from the barrel. The choice may include Boddingtons, Flowers Original, Marston's Pedigree, Morlands Old Speckled Hen and Ringwood Old Thumper. The bar also stocks farm cider and a good selection of wines.

The comprehensive menu, supplemented by daily specials, offers a good choice of home-cooked dishes. From game paté and warm avocado and crispy bacon bake, the menu extends to venison and herb sausages, half-shoulder of lamb with a mint and honey glaze, duck breast in an apricot and cream sauce, fillet steak, and vegetarian dishes like pesto pasta and vegetable curry. Ploughman's lunches and sandwiches are always available.

Children and dogs are welcome inside.

Open from 11.30am till 3pm (Sunday 4pm summer) and from 6pm till 11pm (Monday to Friday 10.30pm winter)

Telephone: (01590) 672158.

Pilley can be reached from the B3054 Beaulieu to Lymington road or from the A337 2 miles north of Lymington.

Approx. distance of walk: 2¾ miles. O.S. Map No. 196 SZ 327/983.

The inn has a small car park to the side plus there is limited space along the lane.

A short but very enjoyable walk on country lanes, through woods and along the banks of the Lymington River. It is generally easy going and dry underfoot - ideal for a warm summer's evening. If you desire a longer walk you can combine this walk with the Hobler at Battramsley; both walks cross at the Red Lion in Boldre.

1. Turn left on leaving the inn and immediately take the arrowed path left beyond the pull-in. Cross the stile in front of you and proceed ahead across the field to a stile and turn right along a lane. At a T-junction turn left and walk along the lane, soon to take the waymarked bridleway on the right, just before the bend beside Southlands School. Follow the drive down towards Vicar's Hill Farm.

2. At the end of the drive go down the grassy path between houses, go over the concrete dive to a gate and descend towards the river. At the bottom turn right and follow the defined path parallel with the river (can be overgrown in summer). Go through a wooden gate on the far side onto a track and turn left. Cross the bridge and walk up to the road junction. Turn right, then at the fork in Boldre village turn right. If you are combining both walks turn left, then left again and go down the lane opposite the Red Lion (turn to page 7).

3. Continue down the hill, over the bridge and turn left into Rodlease Lane. Follow the lane, soon to turn right up the drive to Rodlease Rough Herb Nursery. (Keep to the lane if you wish to visit Boldre Church with its fascinating memorials to H.M.S. Hood). Keep right along the track, then take the arrowed footpath on the right and follow it down into the woods. On reaching a lane turn right and follow it to the T-junction at Pilley Hill. Turn right back to the inn.

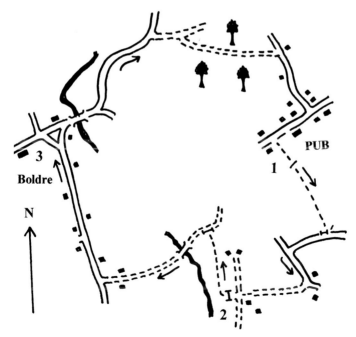

The White Horse (Pub with No Name), Priors Dean

The White Horse, as it does not have an inn sign, is often referred to as 'The Pub with No Name'. It is a wonderful, remotely situated 17th-century farmhouse, full of simple charm, genuinely unspoilt by modernity and surrounded by 13 acres of fields belonging to the pub. Two attractive bars have low-beamed ceilings and real log fires. All the walls are adorned with a large collection of memorabilia, pictures, old clocks, farm implements and pieces of old brass and copper items. To the rear of the building, away from the timeless bars, is a dining room, built in the style of an old barn. Outside there is a secluded garden and a small front terrace with picnic benches.

Although now owned by Gales Brewery, it continues to offers discerning beer drinkers a fine choice of nine real ales, including No Name Best and Strong, Gales HSB, Fuller's London Pride, Hop Back Summer Lightning, Ringwood Fortyniner, Ballards Best and Bass. Country wine lovers have the full range of Gales fruit wines to choose from.

A regularly-changing blackboard lists the range of home-cooked bar food. Typical choice may include beef in ale casserole, Irish stew, lasagne, Cajun chicken, beef and Stilton pie, pork in cider, chicken, ham and leek pie, chilli, as well as sandwiches and hearty ploughman's lunches.

Children are welcome in the dining room; dogs are allowed in on leads only.
Open from 11am till 2.30pm and from 6pm till 11pm.
Telephone: (01420) 588387.

A difficult inn to find! From Petersfield take the A272; just beyond the railway station, turn right at the roundabout towards Steep. In 4 miles, at the East Tisted/ Privett crossroads, turn right and then take the second gravel track right for the inn. Alternatively the inn can be reached from Alton or Winchester via the A32.

Approx. distance of walk: 4¾ miles. O.S. Map No. 197 SU 714/290.

The inn has a large gravel car park.

A lovely peaceful country walk, quite hilly in places but generally easy going. The route is mostly on quiet country lanes and established tracks with a short section on farmland paths. It is best walked during fine weather as a few tracks can be extremely muddy after heavy rain.

1. From the car park go into the field in front of the inn and walk straight across to a stile. Keep ahead through the centre of the field, soon to reach a stile and lane. Turn right and ignore the right turn ahead. Descend steeply, climb to a junction and take the track on your right. Walk past a farm and continue out to the lane. Turn left, gently ascend to a T-junction and turn right.

2. In a few yards take the waymarked 'right of way' on your left and head downhill, steeply at first. Halfway down take the arrowed footpath left to a stile and continue through trees to a stile close to horse jumps. Turn left along the field edge to a stile in the corner and descend steeply through woodland to enter a field. Proceed straight ahead, walk alongside woodland to a road and turn right. Just before a junction, turn right along a track and continue past a house and steeply ascend the path/old lane ahead (can be very muddy).

3. Merge with Warren Lane at the top and continue to a T-junction. Go straight across into the field and follow the good path along the left-hand hedge. With excellent views maintain direction soon to pass farm buildings on your left (John Deere). Keep to the hedge as it bears right, cross a waymarked stile on your left and walk close to the wooden fence. Follow the clear path across the middle of the field to a stile in the far hedge and follow the left-hand edge of the next field back to the inn.

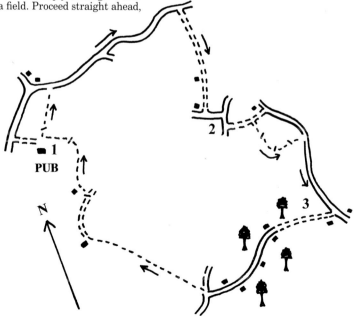

The Rose and Thistle Inn, Rockbourne

Rockbourne must be one of the most enchanting villages in Hampshire, situated amid beautiful rolling downland on the borders of Hampshire, Wiltshire and Dorset. A small brook runs the entire length of the winding village street, which is full of thatched cottages and lovely old period houses. At the north end of the village is the thatched Rose and Thistle, originally built in the 16th century as two cottages before becoming an inn about 180 years ago. Inside, the bar area, originally two rooms now divided by timber props, features an open fire, flagged floors and high-backed wooden settles. The restaurant is dominated by an enormous inglenook fireplace which has roaring log fires in winter. Various pictures and polished brass adorn the walls and the furnishings are old pine and oak settles, tables and chair. The front garden has a terrace with attractive cast-iron and wooden tables with more benches and tables on the lawn.

The inn is a free house dispensing Courage Best, Fuller's London Pride, Adnams Broadside and Marston's Pedigree on handpump.

The inn has an excellent reputation for its food. All dishes are cooked to order and among the light lunchtime favourites you may find elegant Welsh rarebit, tagliatelle carbonara, scrambled egg with smoked salmon and prawns, and roast beef ploughman's. Evening fare is more elaborate, the menu offering duck liver mousse with pistachio nuts and wild mushrooms, rack of lamb with redcurrant sauce, pork fillet with Calvados and cream sauce, and interesting daily specials, notably fresh fish, such as sea bass in lemon butter, monkfish with Oriental sauce, fish pie and Cornish crab salad. Home-made puddings may include bread-and-butter pudding and Bakewell tart.

Children but not dogs are welcome inside the pub.

Open from 11am till 3pm and from 6pm till 11pm.

Telephone: (01725) 518236.

Rockbourne is signposted from the B3078 Fordingbridge to Damerham road, 2 miles west of Fordingbridge. The inn is on the left at the far end of the village.

Approx. distance of walk: 3 miles. O.S. Map No. 184 SU 115/184.

Park behind the inn or at the village hall along the road.

The most westerly walk in the book, a good one for all seasons but best walked on a fine day. Rockbourne is charming village comprising idyllic thatched cottages, a fine 13th-century church, the medieval farm complex of Manor Farm and, just to the south of the village, a Roman Villa and museum. Founded in 1942, the remains of the 40-room villa are the largest in the area (open April to October). Generally easy going, encompassing farmland and woodland path, and quiet country lanes.

1. Leave the inn, turn right and shortly take the lane on the left, signed to the church and Manor Farm. Pass the track on the left for the church (well worth a visit), then keep right at the junction of path, following the farm track through a gate, round to the right and then left through a further gate and over the cattle-grid. Follow the tarmac drive, which soon gives way to gravel, for some distance (ignoring all side tracks), eventually reaching a gate and a lane. Turn left and keep straight on at the cross-roads.

2. At the top of the hill, take the waymarked footpath on the right, just past the post box. Follow the path through woodland, keeping right at a fork of paths to descend through a bluebell wood to reach a lane. Turn right, then left on to an arrowed path beside a house and garden. Gradually climb through the woodland fringe on a defined path, soon to emerge onto a gravel track. Turn right

and, in a few steps, go through the gateway on the left (fingerpost), and walk straight across the field, through a gateway, making for the far corner (yellow arrow on post).

3. Go down the embankment to a junction of tracks. Turn right and keep ahead (you will see a monument on the hill to your left, it was erected to the memory of Sir Eyre Coote who lived in nearby West Park). On reaching the road, turn left then right if wishing to visit the Roman Villa, otherwise go straight across, over the stile and along the path. Pass through two wooden gates and walk beside a house to a further gate and metalled track.

4. Cross the stile almost opposite, pass in front of a thatched cottage to another stile and keep right along the field edge. Climb the stile on the right, bear left along the field edge, passing a barn to reach a drive and small metal gate close to a track. Keep left through a small field, over stile at a crossing of paths and walk across the rear lawns of several cottages to a stile. Cross a small green to a tarmac drive, turn left down to the village street and turn right back to the inn.

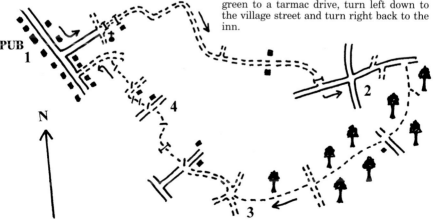

The Coach and Horses, Rotherwick

The residents of Rotherwick are very lucky having an inn as good as the Coach and Horses. The building dates back to the 16th century and although altered over the years it has never lost its character. The two attractively furnished bars have open fireplaces with warm log fires in the winter. At the back is a separate dining room and there are lots of picnic benches at the front surrounded by tubs of flowers in the summer. A small rear patio garden overlooks open farmland.

Owned by Hall & Woodhouse, it specialises in a large range of real ales, namely Badger Best, IPA and Tanglefoot, Wadworth 6X, a guest ale, and two beers from the brewery at the Gribble Inn at Oving (also owned by Hall & Woodhouse) - Reg's Tipple and Blackadder.

Food is served daily and includes a carvery. Blackboards list the range of meals available which may include the usual bar snacks (sandwiches, filled baguettes, ploughman's lunches and soups), plus chilli, lasagne, various pies and pasta dishes, steaks, grilled fish, and puddings like trifle.

No children under 14 in the pub; dogs are welcome.

Open from 11am till 11pm (Sunday 12 noon till 10.30pm).

Telephone: (01256) 762542.

Rotherwick lies to the east of Basingstoke between the A33 and the A30. From the M3 (junction 5) take the B3349 through Hook towards Reading and turn left for Rotherwick in 2 miles.

Approx. distance of walk: 3¾ miles. O.S. Map Nos. 175 and 186 SU 713/563.

Park in the inn's own car park or beside the verge at the front.

An enjoyable short ramble across farmland, through woods and along peaceful country lanes. It is fairly easy going, mostly on dry level ground.

1. Turn right on leaving the inn and, in a short distance, take the signed footpath on the right. Keep straight ahead, at first following the track beside the hedge, and then across the open field, bearing left on the far side to reach a track and crossing of paths. Turn left, then on reaching the road turn right and walk for 200 yards to locate a waymarked footpath on your left into woodland. Shortly, enter a field and keep ahead along the left-hand hedge. Pass through a gap before reaching the road and bear immediately left around field edge, following the defined path back into, and straight through woods to a stile and a road.

2. Go straight across and follow the signed path beside woodland. Climb a stile and continue ahead beside a clearing, bearing left at the end to join a track past houses to a lane. Cross over onto the drive to Wed-man's Farm and after passing through the gate you will see a waymarked footpath on the left beside a brick garage. Follow the fenced path to a stile, then turn right along the field edge and pass through a wooden squeeze-stile on the right. Turn left, go through an old gateway and bear to a further squeeze-stile. Keep right along the field edge, bearing right by a horse jump (old poles) to reach a further squeeze-stile beyond a metal water trough and beside a large oak. Turn left along the field edge to a metal kissing-gate and a lane.

3. Turn right, then left at the Fox Inn and walk down and round the quiet, narrow lane beside woodland, until you reach an opening into a field on the left (fingerpost), just before a house. Turn left and walk round the field edge until you come to a farm track. Turn left and follow it to the road. Cross over, disregard the arrowed path right and follow the track through the farm back to the village lane and the pub opposite.

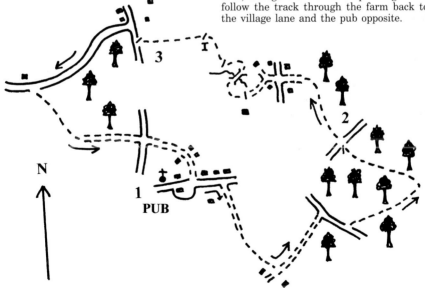

N

1
PUB

The sketch maps in this book are not necessarily to scale but have been drawn to show the maximum amount of detail.

The Woolpack, Sopley

In the middle of Sopley village, beside a tributary of the River Avon, sits the pretty Woolpack Inn. The two-storey thatched pub dates from around the middle of the 18th century. During the last war it was a popular meeting place for the aircrew stationed at nearby R.A.F. Sopley. Various alterations have been carried out since that time but the character of the original inn remains. There is now one main bar with a low-beamed ceiling and open log fires. To one side is a large conservatory dining area. Outside, at the front and beside the stream, are wall-partitioned seating areas, where on a fine day it is very pleasant to sit and watch the antics of the ducks.

It is a Whitbread pub offering three real ales, namely Ringwood Best, Wadworth 6X and Flowers Original.

The Woolpack is a very popular place to eat and can be quite busy, especially at lunchtimes and weekends. There are the usual bar snacks such as sandwiches, ploughman's lunches and salads. The varied main menu may offer smoked salmon with honey, lime and mustard sauce or king prawns in garlic cream for starters, followed by chicken, leek and bacon pie, seafood platter, steak and kidney pudding, mussels steamed in garlic, coriander and cream, lamb steak with mustard and redcurrant sauce, or whole grilled plaice. Puddings range from bannoffee pie and spotted dick, to various ice creams.

Children are well catered for in the family room in the pub. Dogs are also allowed inside.

Open from 11am till 11pm (Sunday 12 noon till 10.30pm).

Telephone: (01425) 672252.

Sopley is situated on the B3347 between Christchurch and Ringwood, $2\frac{1}{2}$ miles north of Christchurch.

Approx. distance of walk: $4\frac{1}{2}$ miles. O.S. Map No. 195 SZ 156/969.

There is a large car park behind the inn; alternatively park in the road opposite which leads to the church.

A splendid country walk - flat, easy going, mostly dry underfoot and ideal for the whole family. It begins by following the Avon Valley Path, a 34 mile-long route that links Christchurch with Salisbury, then traverses farmland via established tracks and well waymarked footpaths.

The Garden at the Woolpack. Walk No. 31

Walk No. 31

1. Leave the inn and turn right in the direction of Ringwood. Just past Sopley Forge, but before reaching a new dwelling, climb a waymarked stile (Avon Valley Path) on the right and follow the course of a stream (dotted with bluebells in spring). Soon climb a stile into a field and proceed ahead, keeping close to the hedge on your right. Cross a further stile on the right and continue along the riverbank and up to a swing-gate beside a bridge.

2. Go straight across the lane and follow the path ahead, beside the stream. Cross a stile into a field and walk ahead to a further stile, then cross the road to follow a short grassy path to a stile. Enter a large field and keep following the right-hand hedge, parallel with the stream until you reach a gap in the hedge. Go through, follow the path round to the left and then right over a concrete bridge into a small field. Proceed ahead on a defined path to a lane.

3. Turn left then immediately right through a small gate to join a well established bridleway. Remain on this long grassy track, at one point crossing a stream, eventually reaching a wooden gate and a gravel track. Follow it round to the right and out through another gate onto a lane. Turn left, then in a few steps bear off right at a junction, soon to take the arrowed footpath right into a copse. Climb a stile on the far side into a field and keep to the right-hand hedge. On the far side bear left along the hedge to locate a gap to cross a bridge and stile.

4. Proceed ahead, then on the far side cross the waymarked stile on the right into a field. Walk round the field, keeping close to the hedge on the right. On the far side climb a stile and continue ahead over a few more stiles, soon to enter a small copse. On the far side is a stile and a wooden bridge over a stream. Keep ahead over one more stile into a field. Ignore the stile on the right and continue ahead until eventually a stile beside a gate leading to a lane.

5. Turn left, then shortly take the track on the left and remain on this as it curves right to reach a staggered crossroads. Go over and walk down the lane opposite. Climb a stile on your left into a field and follow the path around the perimeter until you locate a stile in the hedge on your left. Follow the narrow wooded track and soon merge with a quiet lane. On reaching the one-way system in Sopley, turn right and cross the road to take the little concrete bridge over the river. Turn left along the road back to the inn.

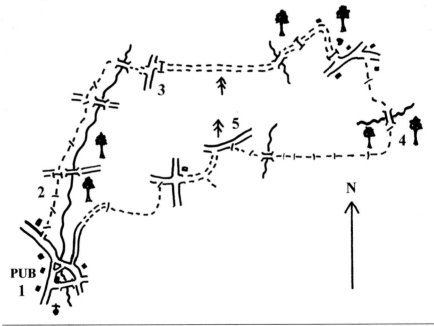

The sketch maps in this book are not necessarily to scale but have been drawn to show the maximum amount of detail.

The Plough Inn, Sparsholt

Located on the edge of the village in one of the most picturesque parts of Hampshire, this much-extended 200-year-old cottage boasts a delightful flower- and shrub-filled garden, complete with children's play houses, chickens and donkeys. The neatly refurbished bar area incorporates the original cottage front rooms and sports pine table, a dresser, comfortable cushioned chairs, an open fire, and attractive prints around the walls.

The Plough is owned by Wadworth and can offer a selection of their real ales, namely Henry's IPA, 6X and a regularly-changing guest ale. Diners will also find a good selection of wines; at least six available by the glass.

Reliable and often imaginative bar is listed on two changing blackboard menus. Dishes range from good pub favourites like cauliflower cheese, salmon and mushroom tagliatelle and lasagne, to interesting meals such as sautéed liver and bacon, leg of lamb steak in juniper and gin, rack of lamb with wild mushrooms, brandy and cream, spicy pork stir-fry, and bourride of fish. A hand-written menu on the bar lists 'doorstop' sandwiches (crab, beef and horseradish), which require a knife and fork to eat!

Children are welcome in the main dining area.

Open from 11am till 3pm and from 6pm till 11pm.

Telephone: (01962) 776353.

Walk No. 32

Sparsholt is situated 2 miles west of Winchester and can be reached from the A3090 Hursley road in the south and the A272 Stockbridge in the north.

Approx. distance of walk: 5½ miles. O.S. Map No. 185 SU 439/314.

The inn has its own large car park.

A delightful, easy going walk starting from the small, quaint village of Sparsholt on quiet country lanes, then following established bridleways through woods and across farmland, passing through Farley Mount Country Park. The woodland paths may be muddy after prolonged rain.

1. Turn right from the pub and bear immediately right, then left down Home Lane, opposite Corner Cottage. At a T-junction turn right, then left at the next bend, signed Moor Court. Follow the lane down and around to a farm at the bottom. Bear right between farm buildings, out onto the rough track beyond. In just over half-a-mile take the arrowed bridleway left, almost opposite a pair of green barns.

2. Proceed straight across a large open field, gently climbing to towards woodland, eventually reaching a small wooden gate where the field narrows to meet the woodland. Enter West Wood and follow the track straight ahead, ignoring any side tracks, to reach open grassland beyond low wooden posts. Bear left up a well defined grassy swathe through Farley Mount Country Park and enter the car park on your left at the top. Walk through the car park, then follow the narrow path at the end parallel with the road. Pass through two more small parking areas and keep to the good path close to the road to reach a Forestry Commission track into West Wood.

3. Turn right to the road and take the arrowed bridleway immediately left into woodland. Follow the path through the woods, ignoring any side turnings, until the path merges with a gravel driveway. At the road go straight across, down the gravel track and follow the footpath ahead until you reach a T-junction of bridleways by an information board (Ham Green). Turn left, then keep left at a fork of ways, walking down to meet a lane at Dean. Bear left uphill and left again at the T-junction for the inn.

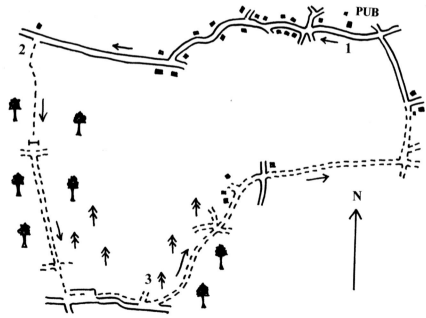

The Harrow, Steep

The Harrow at Steep is a very quaint, two-storey, brick-and-tiled inn tucked peacefully away down a sleepy country lane. Once an old drovers inn, this 400- to 500-year-old building has been in the McCutcheon family since 1929, and it remains a timeless gem, the family keeping it very much as it would have been in the last century (or even earlier?). Inside there are two small rooms, each with boarded walls, scrubbed wooden tables and a hatch-like bar; one has an old brick inglenook fireplace - the place to be on a cold winter's evening. Bundles of dried flowers hang behind the bar above the barrels of beer on their racks.

Now a free house, the Harrow offers a good range of mainly local ales, including Ballards Trotton, Ringwood Best, Flowers Original, Cheriton Brewhouse Best and Diggers Gold.

The menu here is small but very good - everything is home-made on the premises. Expect generously-filled sandwiches, a split-pea- and ham-based soup served with chunks of bread, salads, ploughman's platters, tasty Scotch eggs and, perhaps, home-made quiche and lasagne. Delicious puddings include treacle tart, wild damson Bakewell tart, bread-and-butter pudding and other seasonal creations. Food choice may be limited on Sunday evenings.

Children are not allowed in either bars. Dogs on leads are welcome.

Open 12 noon till 2.30pm (11am till 3pm Saturday) and from 6pm till 11pm. Telephone: (01730) 262685.

Walk No. 33

Steep is situated two miles north of Petersfield and is easily reached from both the A272 and the A3 (Petersfield bypass). From the A3 take the Midhurst turning, turn left at the roundabout, then first left opposite the garage and turn left again at Sheet church to cross A3 to the pub.

Approx. distance of walk: 3½ miles. O.S. Map No. 197 SU 752/252.

There is a small car park opposite the pub, some spaces in the lane outside and spaces up Harrow Lane, a cul-de-sac opposite the lane to the pub.

A most enjoyable short ramble in this beautiful part of East Hampshire. It is quite hilly, fairly dry underfoot, and explores a delightful variety of farmland and woodland paths (rich with bluebells in early summer) and tranquil country lanes.

1. Leave the inn and turn left. Go down to the bottom of the lane, cross the wooden footbridge and follow the path up into beech woods. Emerging on to a narrow lane, turn left and pass a few dwellings to reach a waymarked footpath on your left. Follow a short track and climb a stile beside a gate. Keep close to the fence on the right and follow the field edge left to a stile. Cross a further stile and descend through woodland to meet a track.

2. Turn right into the woodland, the defined and well-waymarked path soon crossing the lawn and drive of a private house back into woodland. Shortly, pass close to large chicken sheds and keep left with marker to cross a stile into a field. Keeping close to the hedge on the right, walk to the far side of the field and beside woodland to a stile. Beyond the stile proceed on a clear path to the left of telegraph poles and bear left uphill to a stile beside a gate. Head steeply uphill on a narrow path to a lane at the top.

3. Turn left along the road (level at first), then descend quite steeply and keep to the lane as it rounds a sharp left bend (small waterfall right). At a road junction, go through the waymarked kissing-gate on the left (Hangers Way) and bear right around the field edge to a stile. Proceed uphill through woodland on a good path, eventually bringing you out onto a grassy area opposite Steep church. At the lane, turn left and follow it right, downhill for half-a-mile back to the inn.

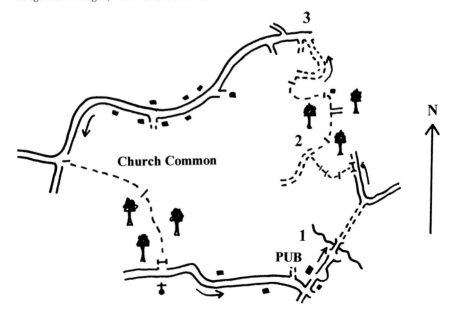

The Mayfly, Testcombe

The Mayfly, a farmhouse dating from 1808, enjoys an idyllic setting right on the banks of the swiftly flowing River Test. With a fine riverside terrace and delightful river scenes, complete with swans and kingfishers, it is a very popular place for a drink or meal, especially at weekends and when the sun shines. Both the traditional bar and conservatory are comfortably furnished and nicely decorated with various fishing regalia around the walls.

A Whitbread Wayside Inn, the Mayfly offers Flowers Original, Boddingtons, Wadworth 6X and Morland Old Speckled Hen on handpump, plus country wines and over ten wines by the glass.

A buffet style food operation copes well with numbers of people that file through past the food counter. Here you can order home-made quiche, hot tandoori chicken, home-cooked ham and an excellent choice of cheeses, then help yourself to the interesting ranges of salads available. Hot daily specials may include game pie, chicken and ham pie, a casserole with dumplings or rack of lamb. Food is served all day everyday from 11.30am till 9.30pm.

Children and dogs are allowed in the pub.

Open from 10am till 11pm.

Telephone: (01264) 860283

Walk No. 34

The inn is situated on the B3057 between Stockbridge and Andover.

Approx. distance of walk: 4 miles. O.S. Map No. 185 SU 382/391.

Park at the inn or over the river bridge at the car park by West Down on the road to Chilbolton.

A beautiful scenic walk through the pretty Test Valley - it is one of my favourites. It crosses both the Test and Anton rivers, traverses farmland and along quiet country lanes. Generally an easy walk following well-waymarked paths and bridleways, notably the Test Way, and is fairly dry underfoot. Ideal for the whole family; there is just one hilly section where a little care is necessary.

1. From the inn turn right, go over the bridge and turn left along the road signed to Chilbolton. Almost immediately take the waymarked Test Way (TW) on your right at the entrance to West Down car park. Follow the distinctive signs up onto West Down and back down to the Chilbolton road nearer the village. Bear left and cross over to follow the (TW) beside a small enclosed green with bench. Follow the narrow enclosed path down towards the river, eventually reaching a playing field. Keep left around the field, leaving via a small gate by some signs to join a gravel track.

2. Pass a cottage and soon bear left on reaching another track. Cross a brook and soon bear off left along a good path to a footbridge, then proceed across lush river meadow to cross two wooden bridges over the delightful River Test to reach a lane. Turn left, ignore the TW arrowed right and continue to take the waymarked bridleway on the right, passing through a gate and under a bridge. Keep to the grassy uphill round the field edge. At the top the path bears right and becomes hedged, eventually reaching a small gate. Cross rough grassland and descend steeply to a gate and cross the main road.

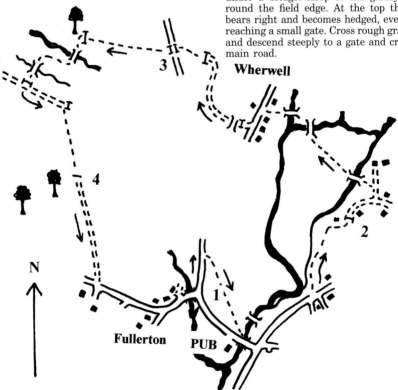

Wherwell

Fullerton   **PUB**

N

3. Go through a gate and follow a bridleway along the field edge to a gate on the far side. Take the arrowed footpath immediately on your left through trees and shortly cross the River Anton. Turn right along a defined path close to the river and cross a stream to reach a metal gate and track. Turn left, then at another gate (private), take the arrowed path right, uphill along the edge of a field and beside woodland to a fence stile at the top.

4. Continue straight ahead along a wide grassy track beside two fields to a lane. Turn left downhill, soon to pass Fullerton Manor and the mill house to reach the A3057. Turn left over the bridge, then in a few yards take the pitted track on your right (postbox). Pass a couple of cottages and join the old railway line. On reaching the road bridge turn left along a narrow path (green arrow - TW) up to a lane and turn right to retrace your steps back over the bridge to the inn.

The Mill House, Fullerton. Walk No. 34

Key to Symbols

road	track	undefined path
stile	bridge	gate
gap in hedge		cattle grid

The sketch maps in this book are not necessarily to scale but have been drawn to show the maximum amount of detail.

The Tichborne Arms, Tichborne

There has been an inn on this site in Tichborne, an idyllic hamlet nestling in the peaceful Itchen Valley, since the 16th century, although the present attractive inn dates only from 1939 having been built after the second of two major fires. In common with most of the buildings in the village the pub is cloaked with a heavy thatch, making both a favoured destination. The well tended and sheltered rear garden is a popular spot for warm weather imbibing. Inside, there are two bars, the Hampshire, simply furnished with direct access to the garden, and the smaller, panelled and more comfortable Tichborne Bar.

Expect a warm welcome at this free house and real ale dispensed straight from casks behind the bar. The choice includes Flowers IPA, Wadworth 6X and Fuggle Imperial.

The inn offers a good choice of bar snacks plus several daily specials. Everthing except the bread is home-made and cooked on the premises. You can choose from a tasty soup (watercress), chicken liver paté, fillet jacket potatoes (prawns, cheese and garlic butter), ploughman's lunches, salads, freshly-prepared sandwiches and toasties. The changing specials may include liver, bacon and onion casserole, steak, ale and Stilton pie, fish pie, chicken breast with apricots and brandy, chilli and goulash. Lemon cheesecake, syrup sponge, meringues with chocolate, and bread-and-butter pudding appear on the pudding list.

Children are not allowed inside the pub. Dogs are very welcome.

Open from 11.30am till 2.30pm and from 6pm till 11pm.

Telephone: (01962) 733760.

Picturesque Tichborne lies just south of Alresford and is easily accessible from the A31 (signposted) and the A272 via Cheriton.

Approx. distance of walk: 6 miles. O.S. Map No. 185 SU 571/305.

Park in the pub car park or by the church.

A gently undulating and peaceful ramble through lovely open countryside around the Itchen Valley. Tichborne is a charming thatched village and St Andrews Church is well worth visiting for the interesting historical booklet about this fascinating village. Some of the tracks and field paths can be very muddy after wet weather.

1. Turn left from the inn and take the track on the right at the sharp left-hand bend. Almost immediately go left up a grassy path to drive in front of the church. Bear left past the Old School House and turn right along a high-hedged track. Emerge into a field and keep to the track along its left-hand hedge. Follow the path along the hedge at the end of the track and soon cross a stile on your left. Bear right towards a barn, climbing a stile onto a track.

2. Turn right and gently ascend, passing a further barn to reach a fork of track. Bear left through the smaller of two gates and keep left along the field edge, soon to climb to a stile on the woodland fringe at the top of the field. The path winds its way through this bluebell wood to reach a metalled track. Continue ahead down the lane, then where the track bears right towards a farm, keep ahead down a stony bridleway into Hill Houses. Pass a couple of thatched cottages on your left, then just past garages take the waymarked footpath left up a track beside a house.

3. Keep to the path beside the right-hand hedge, cross a stile on your right and walk along the field edge towards a pylon. Bear half left across the field, keeping to the left of the pylon to locate a gap in the hedge, then turn right and walk round the field edge to a rough farm track. Turn right, go though the farm by Sevington Manor and cross straight over a road onto a further track. Cross the River Itchen, then on entering a field keep to the right-hand hedge to a stile. Do not cross the stile, turn left and follow the defined path to a stile beside a gate at a belt of trees. Climb a further stile and keep ahead across parkland to a stile by the gates to Tichborne House.

4. Proceed straight ahead (private road left), then where the tarmac estate road bears left, keep ahead along a gravel track. As this enters woodland (private), bear off right along a grassy track, then along the left-hand edge of a field, eventually crossing two stiles onto a track above the Alresford bypass. Turn left, the path bearing left to reach Vernal Farm. Follow the farm track across the river and road and ascend a good path along the left-hand edge of a field (Itchen Way). At the top, bear left with the defined wide path, following left down the field edge towards Tichborne Church. Remain on this track into the village, turning left at the road back to the inn.

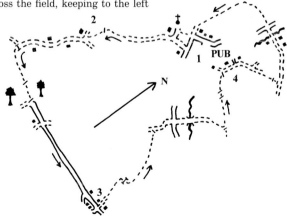

The Bear and Ragged Staff, Timsbury

The Bear and Ragged Staff is a friendly, 'Wayside' inn, occupying a rural position close to the River Test. The interesting inn sign is presumed to be based on the Earl of Warwick's coat of arms, on which the bear and ragged staff is depicted. As well as a rest area and a good children's play area, there's a large seating area inside where all tables, including some very heavy elm ones, are individually named. One wall of the main bar is dominated by a large open fireplace. To the rear of the pub are plenty of picnic-type tables and chairs.

The inn is owned by Whitbread and five real ales are offered, including Fuggles IPA, Flowers Original, Boddingtons, Greene King Abbot Ale and a regularly-changing guest beer.

Food is available all day everyday (12 noon till 9.30pm; 10pm Saturday); you can choose from the printed menu or pick one of the daily specials chalked up on the blackboard. From favourite snacks like Stilton ploughman's, Wayside Inn platter (ham sandwich and soup) and hot chicken and bacon salad, the menu extends to lemon chicken, liver, ale and onions, steak and ale pie, salmon bearnaise, and such specials as trout stuffed with prawns and horseradish, and fillet of pork with prunes and fruit compote. Puddings include treacle pudding and chocolate fudge cake. There is also a separate children's menu.

The inn is open all day from 11am till 11pm (12 noon till 10.30pm Sundays).

Telephone: (01794) 368602.

The inn is located beside the A3057 Romsey to Stockbridge road, 3 miles north of Romsey.

Approx. distance of walk: 4½ miles. O.S. Map No. 185 SU 335/258.

The inn has two car parks.

A beautiful scenic walk through the lovely Test Valley - one of my favourites. The walk is hilly in places, fairly dry underfoot and easy to follow. It takes you across fields, through woods, back and forth over the River Test, down country lanes, along the Test Way and through the grounds of Mottisfont Abbey (a 12th-century Augustinian Priory) and historic Mottisfont village, both owned by the National Trust.

1. Start from the front of the inn and go the lane towards Michelmersh. Near the top, where you meet another lane, turn left and continue to the next T-junction. Proceed straight across through the gates and up the drive (waymarker post), past a fine thatched cottage, keeping left to enter a field. Follow the path across the centre of the field into a grassy area, passing to the left of some barns and shortly reach another field. A fingerpost directs you half-left across the field, passing the telegraph pole (yellow arrow) to the edge of woodland, then bear diagonally left downhill to waymarker on the edge of a copse. Descend steeply through a thicket to a stile and bear right across a field to a stile beside a gate.

2. Cross the main road, go through the fencing and down the tarred drive and keep straight ahead to cross the River Test. Climb the stile (by a gate) ahead into a meadow and follow the defined path (white-topped posts) to reach a stile bridge and gravel track on the far side. Turn left, pass some cottages and continue round, over the bridge and past some buildings to a kissing-gate set in the hedge on your left (Test Way). Bear half-right across the field to a group of oaks, then continue on the defined path in the same direction to a waymarker by a large tree. Bear right and follow the path up to a kissing-gate (good views of Mottisfont Abbey to your left), and turn left along the lane into Mottisfont village.

3. Follow the road left past the the the Old Post Office (tea-rooms) and take the turning on the right to the church which dates from 676 AD. To visit the Abbey and gardens keep

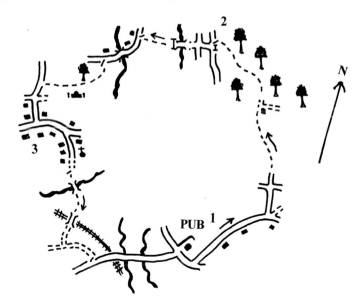

Walk No. 36

ahead to the main entrance - open April to October from Saturday to Wednesday 12-6pm (Rose garden & grounds daily 12-8.30pm in June). The lane past the church eventually merges with a grass-centred track leading down to a gate and a field. Climb the waymarked stile and follow the clear path ahead to a wooden bridge over the River Dun. Cross the river and go up the fenced path into the woods. Cross the railway bridge and remain on the track, then at a crossing of tracks turn left and walk down to a stile and the road. Turn left over the level crossing and keep to the road back to the main road and the inn opposite.

The River Test. Walk No. 36

The Brushmakers Arms, Upham

The Brushmakers Arms is an interesting old pub: the building dates back some 600 years and has alternated between being a pub and a brushmaker's workshop. I am reliably informed that Cromwell once stayed here while his men were garrisoned up the road. The inn is also reputed to have its own resident ghost. Today it is a quaint, comfortable and well decorated pub with one main bar and an adjoining dining area, both heated by the same real fire in winter. The walls are adorned with a collection of different brushes. To the rear is a lovely lawn and terrace with picnic benches and colourful tubs of flowers.

Being a free house the inn offers a selection of real ales, including Bass, Ringwood Best, Brush Bitter and a changing guest ale.

A good food menu is available daily, including hearty snacks like freshly-cut sandwiches, ploughman's lunches, jacket potatoes and home-made soups. Lunchtime visitors can tuck into home-made lasagne, curry, cod and chips, rump steak, or choose from one of the interesting vegetarian dishes on offer. The evening a la carte menu (served Wednesday to Saturday) offers the full range of dishes, including fish, steaks and pork. For pudding there may be home-made pavlova, custard tart or lemon meringue.

Children are welcome away from the bar

Open from 11am till 2.30pm (3pm Saturday; 3.30pm Sunday) and from 5.30pm till 11pm.

Telephone: (01489) 860231.

Walk No. 37

Upham is best reached from the B3037 & B2177 between Eastleigh and Bishop's Waltham. Take the unclass road north at Lower Upham (near the junction of the two B-roads), 2 miles north-west of Bishops Waltham.

Approx. distance of walk: 3¾ miles. O.S. Map No. 185 SU 540/206.

Parking is limited to the lane outside the inn or in the lane by the duck pond.

Upham is a pretty, isolated village surrounded by peaceful rolling countryside. The walk explores scenic farmland paths, wide established tracks and quiet village lanes; all affording unspoilt rural views. It is ideal for the whole family, although there is one steep climb near the end.

1. Turn right on leaving the pub, then right again at the junction opposite the pond and walk through the village. Where the lane bears sharp left turn right and shortly climb the waymarked stile on the left, beyond Manor Cottage. Cross the field and the stile in the fence opposite and bear left around the field edge on a grassy path. In the far left-hand corner join a belt of trees and keep ahead at the junction, soon to descend across a field to a small copse and a stile. Bear diagonally left uphill across a field to a stile and turn left along the field edge (Monarch's Way). In a few paces, at a junction of routes, take the blue arrowed bridleway across the centre of a large field, eventually reaching a gravel track.

2. Turn right along the track, keep right at a junction of paths, skirting the edge of woodland. Remain on this track as it bears right away from the wood and uphill between fields. The track narrows to a flinty path towards the top of Green Hill, leading to a gate, a track and a lane. Turn right, pass houses on the right and soon bear off right along a waymarked bridleway (second of two paths). Lookout for and take the arrowed path right through the hedge and keep ahead to follow a wide grassy track (hedge on your left) downhill towards Woodlock's Down Farm.

3. Cross the metalled drive and stile opposite. Shortly, at a junction of paths, turn left along a track. Where this bends left (private sign), bear off right across the centre of a field on a defined path. Walk through a copse and turn right around the field edge on the far side. Follow it left (yellow arrows) and steeply uphill, bearing left on a good path through trees at the top to reach a lane at the top of White Hill. Turn right into Upham, bearing left at the small green and junction back to the inn.

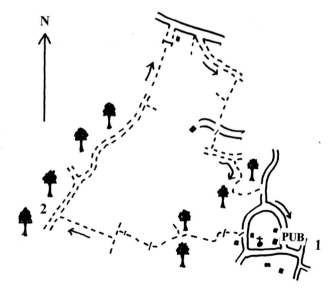

N

The Hoddington Arms, Upton Grey

Tucked away in an extremely pretty village close to Basingstoke and within easy reach of the M3, the unpretentious and welcoming Hoddington Arms, formerly two farm cottages, dates from the 18th century. You will find two neat and inviting beamed bars, both traditionally furnished, and a delightful rear garden and patio with tables and chairs for fine weather drinking.

The Hoddington Arms is a Morland pub offering their own Old Speckled Hen and IPA ales plus Ruddles Best and a regularly-changing guest beer such as Bass and Flowers Original.

Blackboards list the extensive choice of food available (not Sunday evenings) in the popular dining areas. Both the bar menu and the carte list a good range of steaks, local game and fresh fish to satisfy all tastes. From the bar menu you may choose Stilton and mushrooms on toast, ploughman's lunches, freshly-cut sandwiches (not Sunday lunchtime), filled jacket potatoes, steak and kidney pie, game casserole, venison and port, Hoddington fish bake, honeyed lamb casserole, creamy pork with peppers, and chicken and mushroom pie. Puddings may include raspberry flan, 'sexy' apple pie, chocolate fudge cake and lemon meringue pie.

Children are welcome in the family room.

Open from 11.30am till 2.30pm and from 6pm till 11pm; food is served between 12 noon and 2pm and from 7pm till 9pm (except Sunday evenings).

Telephone: (01256) 862371.

Walk No. 38

Upton Grey is signposted and easily reached from the B3349 Odiham to Alton road at South Warnborough. It is also signposted from the A32 just south of Basingstoke and from the A30 at Basing, 1 mile east of the M3 (J6).

Approx. distance of walk: 5 miles. O.S. Map No. 186 SU 700482.

The inn has a car park.

From the attractive village of Upton Grey, complete with fine manor houses, thatched cottages, unusual Norman church, and a duck pond, this gently undulating ramble explores the rolling farmland, woods and tracks that characterise this unspoilt downland area close to Basingstoke and the M3. Take time to visit the small church at Weston Patrick with its simple 12th-century doorway.

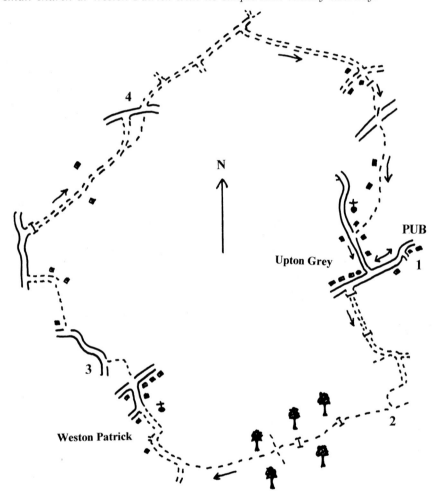

The sketch maps in this book are not necessarily to scale but have been drawn to show the maximum amount of detail.

1. From the inn turn left along the road, passing the duck pond and main village street. Just past Weston Close and opposite Orton House, take the waymarked footpath left through a gate. Follow defined track uphill beside the left-hand fence to a gate. Keep to the track, then at a fingerpost disregard footpath right and bear left with the track into woodland. At a branch of tracks keep ahead. Then at the top of the field follow the track left then right around the field edge to a T-junction of paths.

2. Turn right and soon enter woodland by a gate (yellow arrow). Keep to the main path through pheasant enclosures and leave via a similar gate. At a crossing of tracks keep straight ahead through woodland, then follow good path across an open field. Join a track and keep ahead, downhill to farm buildings and a small metal gate, ignore stile left and follow track round Weston Patrick church and down through hamlet to a road. Cross straight over and follow defined path along left-hand edge of field, bearing left with hedge to pass farm buildings to a lane.

3. Turn right, then in a short distance where the road curves left, take the arrowed path right beside a house into a field. Proceed straight ahead, uphill parallel with telegraph poles towards a house, soon to bear left along a track in front of the house to reach a lane. Turn right and soon bear off right (waymarked), passing beside gates on to a wide track. Remain on this track which soon becomes a metalled drive leading to a road. Just before it bends left to the road, keep ahead on path and cross the road on to an arrowed 'right of way'.

4. With good views keep to this track. Take the second track right (just before barn) and follow this to a junction of tracks on edge of village. Bear left, then almost immediately right along short path to a stile. Bear half-right across paddock to a stile, cross a lane following path along field edge and down close to farm buildings and between dwellings to reach the main street in Upton Grey. Turn left, then left again at the pond back to the inn.

£4.95

£4.95

91

The George Inn, Vernham Dean

High up in northern Hampshire, close to the Wiltshire and Berkshire borders is the isolated village of Vernham Dean. The pretty George Inn, a friendly village local, built in the 16th century has timbered brick and flint walls supporting an attractive tiled roof which curves around the upper storey windows. Inside there are three inter-connecting bars, each with its own fireplace and large log fires in winter, and all have heavily timbered walls and beamed ceilings. The furnishings are simple, comfortable and in keeping with the rest of the inn. Outside there are a couple of picnic benches and a lawned beer garden to the rear.

Marston's Brewery own the inn and serve their Best Bitter, Pedigree and Head Brewer's Choice Ale, and Bank's Mild on handpump.

Good bar food is available daily. The menu, chalked up on the blackboard, changes daily and well feature garlic mushrooms, king prawns in filo pastry and fresh moules for starters, followed by home-cooked ham, egg and chips, steak and kidney pie, chicken curry, battered cod and decent steaks served with a variety of sauces (Dijon mustard, pepper, onions and garlic). Interesting special dishes of the day may include kleftico (Greek lamb dish), Italian chicken casserole and lamb with mustard sauce. Vegetarians are well catered for and a roast in served on Sunday lunchtimes.

Children are welcome inside if they are eating and dogs are allowed in on leads only.

Open from 11.30am till 3pm and from 6pm till 11pm.

Telephone: (01264) 737279.

Vernham Dean is best reached from the A343 Andover to Newbury road. Take the turning for Upton at Hurstbourne Tarrant and continue up valley to reach the village; the George is on the right after the school.

Approx. distance of walk: 3½ miles. O.S. Map No. 174 SU 342/566.

The inn has its own car park to the front. Alternatively park at the village hall or by the playing field along the lane to the left of the inn.

Vernham Dean is a lovely peaceful village in the most north-westerley tip of Hampshire. The walk is easy, mostly across farmland, but there is one steep climb up through a meadow. The effort is rewarded by splendid views across the rolling 'Hampshire Highlands' towards Inkpen Beacon.

1. Leave the inn and turn right. Walk past the shop and turn left up a gravel track beside a house called Underwood. Cross the stile beside the gate, then keep left where the tracks forks, along the field edge towards woodland. Follow the waymarked path left into the wood and keep to the main path, eventually emerging into a meadow. Bear left and keep close to the woods on your left. Ascend steeply, following the small wooden posts, and soon pass through the gap in a thicket into a field. Bear right and walk straight across the centre of the field to an opening in the far hedge and a lane.

2. Turn left and follow this narrow lane with very little traffic downhill to a T-junction. Go straight across the stile opposite and bear diagonally left across the field to an opening in the hedge opposite. Go up the field, following the line of telegraph poles, and bear left at the top. Keep to the field edge and soon take the arrowed path off to the right into a small wooded copse. Pass to the rear of a house, cross the drive to a gate and walk through the churchyard, exiting onto a lane via a gate. Turn left, then left again at the junction and follow the lane for ¾ mile back to the village and the inn.

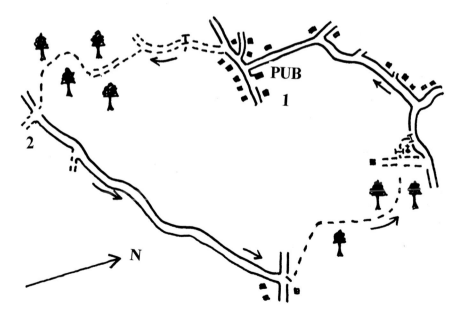

The sketch maps in this book are not necessarily to scale but have been drawn to show the maximum amount of detail.

The Cartwheel, Whitsbury

The Cartwheel must surely be everyone's idea of the ideal country pub. Situated in the tranquil village of Whitsbury, in an area of outstanding natural beauty, it was originally two cottages built in 1796. Around 1860 it became an inn and was just known as the Wheel. At that time it was supplied with beer from Carter's Brewery in Ringwood. There is one main cosy bar with an open fireplace, a separate games room and a cosy candlelit dining room seating up to twenty. Outside you'll find a lovely beer garden with a summer barbeque area and a children's play area.

The bar is well stocked with a large range of drinks; six handpumps dispense a good range of real ales - Adnams Broadside, Ringwood Fortyniner and, perhaps, Fullers London Pride, Smiles Best and Hopback Summer Lightning. Over 30 real ales are featured at the annual beer festival in August. You will also find two ciders and a wide selection of Continental bottled lagers.

There is an extensive blackboard menu catering for all tastes, including children and vegetarians. Interesting home-cooked dishes range from ploughman's lunches, sandwiches and vegetarian dishes like roasted peppers stuffed with mushroom risotto and cashew nut paella, to chicken liver parfait, Cumberland sausages and mash, steak and kidney pudding, grilled cod with pesto Lancashire hotpot, pork chops with black pudding, venison casserole with redcurrants, and good steaks. Round off with banoffee pie, rhubarb crumble or strawberry and banana trifle. Food is served daily, except Tuesday evenings between October and April.

Children and dogs are welcome indoors

Open from 11am till 2.30pm (3pm Saturday) and from 6pm till 9pm. Usual Sunday hours.

Telephone: (01725) 518362.

Whitsbury is best reached from Fordingbridge off the B3078. The inn is in the main street in the centre of the village.

Approx. distance of walk: 5 miles. O.S. Map No. 184 SU 128/188.

The inn has a large car park.

Whitsbury is a lovely tranquil village, beautifully kept and surrounded by delightful downland scenery. It is famous for its racing stables, notably Whitsbury Manor Stud which has bred and trained several Grand National winners, the most famous being Desert Orchid and Rhyme and Reason. Although quite long the walk is easy going, following mainly established tracks and passes through the historic grounds of Breamore House (with its ancient miz-maze).

1. From the inn turn right and walk up through the village to the stables at the top of the hill. Take the waymarked bridleway along the metalled drive between white paddock fencing, following it right, then left onto a wide grassy track that heads downhill, passing beside a gate. At the bottom, cross the track and the stile opposite and walk up the field on a wide track, soon to skirt woodland to reach a junction and a barn. Keep left through the woods, out through the gateway on the far side and follow the grassy track beside the right-hand fence to a stile and junction of tracks.

2. Turn right and follow the bridleway past woodland on your right (permissive paths to view the ancient miz-maze), then on reaching a gravel track bear left, then right and follow the track down through Breamore Wood (carpeted with bluebells in spring and red campion and foxgloves in summer). Pass Breamore House (open most afternoons Easter to September), then as you leave via the main gates, turn right along the gravel track, passing the tea rooms, Countryside Museum and charming thatched cottages to reach a lane. Continue ahead through Upper Street and turn right along Rookery Lane.

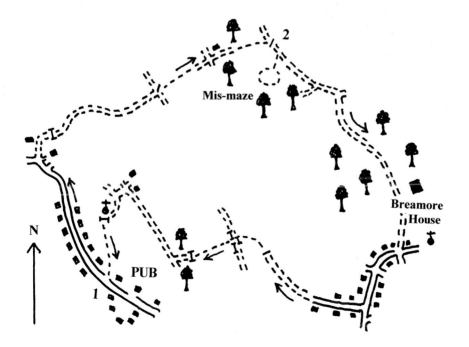

Walk No. 40

3. Just beyond a thatched cottage the lane merges into a track. Proceed straight ahead until you reach a stile beside a gate. Follow the path along a gulley beside a field, downhill to a gate and track. Turn right, then almost immediately left through the metal gate and follow the waymarked bridleway uphill along the field edge to a gate on the edge of woodland. Walk through the woods, keeping right at a fork, soon to follow the wide path between paddocks and woodland. On reaching a bungalow, take the track on the left between paddocks and bear left round to the church. Go through the gate into the churchyard, walk round the church and out through the small gate. Follow the path down to the village lane and turn left back to the inn.

Breamore House. Walk No. 40

Key to Symbols

========= road   :::::::::: track   ---------- undefined path

✓ stile   ⤙⤚ bridge   ├───┤ gate

─┤ ├─ gap in hedge   ⊟ cattle grid

The sketch maps in this book are not necessarily to scale but have been drawn to show the maximum amount of detail.